Building Influence in the Workplace

BUILDING INFLUENCE IN THE WORKPLACE

HOW TO GAIN AND RETAIN INFLUENCE AT WORK

Aryanne Oade
Director, Oade Associates Limited

First published 2010 by
PALGRAVE MACMILLAN

Palgrave Macmillan in the UK is an imprint of Macmillan Publishers Limited, registered in England, company number 785998, of Houndmills, Basingstoke, Hampshire RG21 6XS.

Palgrave Macmillan in the US is a division of St Martin's Press LLC, 175 Fifth Avenue, New York, NY 10010.

Palgrave Macmillan is the global academic imprint of the above companies and has companies and representatives throughout the world.

Palgrave® and Macmillan® are registered trademarks in the United States, the United Kingdom, Europe and other countries

ISBN 978–0–230 –23773–5

This book is printed on paper suitable for recycling and made from fully managed and sustained forest sources. Logging, pulping and manufacturing processes are expected to conform to the environmental regulations of the country of origin.

A catalogue record for this book is available from the British Library.

A catalog record for this book is available from the Library of Congress.

10 9 8 7 6 5 4 3 2 1
19 18 17 16 15 14 13 12 11 10

Printed and bound in Great Britain by the
MPG Books Group, Bodmin and Kings Lynn

About the Author

Aryanne Oade has worked as a Chartered Psychologist since 1991. She has appeared on Channel 4 television speaking about customer complaints handling, has given an address on 'Creativity in Business' at the British Association for the Advancement of Science, and has appeared on Radio 4 speaking on the same topic. Aryanne has spoken at the Leeds and York Institute of Directors Breakfast Meetings on 'Politics, Power and Profit,' and at the British Psychological Society's Annual Conference on 'Stress Levels Among South Yorkshire Probation Officers.' She is a member of the British Psychological Society's Special Group in Coaching Psychology, and holds general membership at the Society's Division of Occupational Psychology. Aryanne is also a member of the Association for Coaching.

Note from the Author

This book focuses on your influencing skills and how you apply them at work when handling a range of colleagues and co-workers. In writing the book, I am not seeking to advise you, the reader, on how to handle your workplace relationships, but rather to offer you my experience and know-how as someone who has coached and worked with hundreds of clients on these issues. In addition to reading this book, you might want to seek the services and professional advice of a coach, business psychologist or consultant, each of whom should be able to offer you tailored, detailed and impartial counsel on the more challenging inter-personal and influencing issues you might face at work.

Acknowledgments

I would like to acknowledge a number of people who have played a part in my work and the writing of this book.

Firstly, my thanks and gratitude go to all the clients who have spoken with me about their experiences of seeking to gain and retain influence at work. I am grateful to the many clients who have shared with me their successes, frustrations, reactions, and strategies for managing – and using – influential behavior in the workplace. These are perhaps the most frequently recurring concerns that clients bring to coaching meetings, and the ones that most often see them making rapid progress back at the workplace.

Next, I would like to thank the clients and contacts who allowed me to pick their brains at the start of the writing process for this book. These conversations were valuable to me, helping me to decide how to structure and focus its chapters. I send my thanks to each one of you gratefully and anonymously.

Then, I'd like to send my appreciation to Julie Perry and Gina Rowland for their helpful critique of the early chapters of the book; and to Arthur Soar for his feedback towards the end of the writing process.

Finally, I'd like to acknowledge the contribution of Stephen Rutt and the team at Palgrave Macmillan for their effective collaboration through the production process.

Overview

WHAT THIS BOOK IS ABOUT

This book is about personal influence at work: what it is, how to gain it, how to retain it, and how to use the influence you have already attained to get things done. It is about your ability to acquire and sustain influence with colleagues with whom you have some shared values and some things in common, as well as being about building and retaining influence with colleagues with whom you have no shared values and very little in common.

The book examines how to build influence with the colleagues you meet every day in your team or department, as well as how to build influence with your organization's opinion-formers and decision-makers, colleagues with whom you might meet infrequently and for short intervals only. The book will help you to understand your own values as an influencer, and enable you to recognize the links between 'having influence,' 'having power' and 'having responsibility.' It considers how to position your influencing arguments with colleagues who have different values from you and who won't be influenced by the factors which readily influence you. It examines how to build influence with irresponsible colleagues and with colleagues who want you to behave in ways that conflict with your wishes. It explores effective ways of raising your profile outside of your department, and effective ways of building influence with internal clients and senior managers. It will equip you with strategies, tactics, techniques and know-how so that you can learn how to consistently use behavior that proves persuasive with all your colleagues and workplace contacts.

The book is written for people at work at any level of an organization in any part of the world. The book outlines the principles for creating and maintaining influential relationships at work, and those principles are relevant across the board. So, whether you work for a small, medium or large organization and no matter which continents you work in, this book should help you to become a more influential member of your organization's workforce.

WHY I WROTE THIS BOOK

I wrote this book for the very many of you who go to work and need to get things done in tandem with others in order to be effective in your roles. The main sets of skills you need to be effective day in, day out are influencing skills. You can't use authority to get things done when you work with your peers or your managers, and it isn't considered wise to do so with your team members except when you really need to. On a day-to-day basis you will have to find another way to get done the things you need to get done. You need to go to work every day and establish and maintain effective, influential connections with your colleagues, some of whom you may not naturally like or want to work with, but with whom you need to gain and retain influence if you are to succeed.

In many organizations it's the unofficial connections between people that determine what decisions get made, which projects receive funding and support, which ideas receive sponsorship, who gets promoted and even who gets hired and fired. Learning how to build and retain influential relationships with your colleagues is a key component of organizational life, but most people have to work out for themselves how to do it effectively. It's not part of the induction program. I wrote this book for those of you who want to speed up the process of gaining influence with key colleagues, as well as for those of you who want to know how to retain the influence you already have and use it to help you achieve the goals and objectives that matter to you.

I wrote the book out of a firm conviction that being technically able at your role often isn't enough to build a reputation at work. It's OK as a starting point, but is no more than that. I believe that most frequently it's the quality of the relationships you build with your colleagues that will determine how effective you are perceived to be. And many people working in organizations today have had very little or no development in the influencing and people-handling skills they need to enable them to engage productively with and work effectively alongside a range of colleagues and co-workers. Without the ability to build influential relationships with your colleagues, retain influence with them and use the influence you do have to get things done, you may well not be seen as an influential member of the workforce even if your knowledge base and technical skills might suggest you could be.

BUILDING INFLUENCE AT WORK

If you want to have influence in the workplace it is vital that you develop and hone an effective set of influencing skills, tactics and strategies from which to select when handling different people, issues and personalities. Your suite of influencing tools needs to be sufficiently well developed that you have options when interacting with, interpreting and responding to the many different people around you. It needs to provide you with choices for handling managers more senior than you, colleagues who are your peers and those who work at a more junior level to you.

Your suite of influencing skills also needs to enable you to handle people with whom you share objectives and values as well as those people who want different things from you and whose methods of getting things done are very different from yours. It must also help you handle those colleagues skilled at appearing to be productive while not achieving very much at all, as well as managing those colleagues who want you to supply the energy, ideas, or strategies they subsequently pass off as their own.

This book will help you to become more accomplished at all these things. It will equip you with the insight, self-awareness, know-how, skills and knowledge that will enable you to:

- **Recognize and manage the impact of your influencing style on other people.**
- Read other people's influencing styles effectively.
- Select and apply the most useful and effective influencing strategies and tactics in a range of key situations.

MY BACKGROUND AND WORKPLACE EXPERIENCE

I am a Chartered Psychologist. I began working as a business psychologist in the late 1980s. During the following five years I worked for three consultancy firms before deciding to work as an independent business psychologist in early 1994. I made this move because I wanted to spend the greater part of my time working directly with clients, rather than managing colleague relationships. Some of my initial projects were carried out as an associate to smaller consultancy firms. Then, in January 2000, I set up Oade Associates to design and deliver bespoke executive coaching programmes, tailored professional skills workshops and custom-made conference scenarios.

In this work I combine business psychology with the skills of professional actors. We create real-life scenarios that reflect the leadership and influencing, negotiating and conflict-resolution, political management and people-handling issues that my clients deal with in their day-to-day work. Since starting Oade Associates, I have run hundreds of executive coaching programs and professional skills workshops for managers and leaders working in the United Kingdom, Europe and North America. Many of these projects have involved working with clients on the reality of building, retaining and using influence at work.

In my coaching programs and workshops I ask clients to step back from their day-to-day work and workplace experiences. I ask them to reflect on the quality of the influencing behavior they use when things are going well for them, and to compare that with what they do when they are under pressure. Then, with the help of my professional actor colleagues, I recreate the very meetings clients find most challenging, meetings that they mishandle or in which they lose influence or credibility, and help clients to revisit these meetings using different and more productive influencing behavior, skills and tactics. I coach them to understand the links between their intra-personal world – their values, character and personality – and their inter-personal behavior: the influencing tactics, skills and strategies they use with other people. Clients practice their new influencing approaches until they are satisfied that they can go back to work and use them straight away. As a result of working in this way clients perform better in their roles, have greater influence in their key workplace relationships and demonstrate sustained behavior change.

In addition to working one-to-one and with small groups I also work with conference audiences. In this case I develop a series of custom-made sketches which my actor colleagues subsequently enact live on stage. Audience members discuss and debate the action at round tables, so that they can learn from one another's experiences of handling similar instances, and decide which inter-personal skills and tactics work well in particular situations and which don't. Scenarios have focused on managing the boundaries between colleagues' personal and private lives, handling under-performing colleagues and responding to perceived harassment and sexism at work.

This book comes out of my experience of helping hundreds of clients to develop the influencing skills they need to perform effectively in their roles, and out of my belief that it is the quality of a person's people-handling skills that largely determines who will gain and retain true influence in the workplace.

How To Use This Book

WHO THIS BOOK IS FOR

I wrote the book for those of you who want to understand what practical actions you can take to become a more influential member of your team, department or organization.

Some of you simply may not know how to go about gaining influence. In this case you may be someone who:

- Has excellent technical knowledge but lacks the people-handling skills you need to develop your reputation beyond your immediate team.
- Knows your stuff but struggles to get senior, more influential people to listen to your ideas and proposals.
- Knows what needs to be done, but has difficulty convincing other people to sponsor your plans or take on board what you are saying.
- Has great ideas but doesn't know how to sell the merits of your proposals to your colleagues, and may sadly fail to get the level of profile your suggestions deserve.
- Works very hard but does not get the opportunities or rewards that your skill, effort and commitment merit.

I wrote this book for those of you who identify with any or all of these situations. I also wrote this book for those of you who don't know how to take advantage of the opportunities to influence that you already do have. You may:

- Struggle to select and use behavior which proves influential with key senior colleagues or key peers when you meet with them.
- Be unable to actively manage the perceptions you create in the minds of your key workplace contacts and fail to secure their good opinion even when you have something valuable to say.
- Not recognize the negative impact that your current influencing style has on some of your colleagues.
- Fail to select and use the most influential arguments in the ad hoc or more formal meetings you have with senior people, where what you say is just as important as how you say it.

WHAT THIS BOOK WILL DO FOR YOU

This book will take you through a process of stepping back from your day-to-day work and considering how you go about influencing key colleagues in the workplace. It will help you to reevaluate how you initiate and respond to opportunities to exert influence at work, and encourage you to reassess how you build influence with your key workplace contacts.

The book will introduce you to a series of case studies and smaller examples, each of which mirrors realistic workplace influencing dynamics. These case studies and smaller examples will illustrate the pitfalls, mistakes, oversights, and errors of judgment that can lose you influence and harm your credibility. They will also provide a blueprint for how to go about maximizing the influence you could have in a range of key workplace situations.

As you read the book you will be encouraged to step back from your day-to-day work and:

- Review how you currently seek to influence a range of your key workplace contacts.
- Identify your areas of strength and your areas for development as an influencer.
- Make decisions about what to do to improve the way in which you set about influencing your key workplace contacts.

Periodically, the book contains a series of questions for you to consider and answer in relation to your experiences of seeking to build influence at work. Each question is followed by a space in the text so that you can jot down your answers to it if you want to. These questions will provide you with an opportunity to apply the key points from the previous sections of the book to your working life, helping you get the most out of the process of reading the material.

THE CASE STUDIES AND SMALLER EXAMPLES

From Chapter 1 onwards, the book will introduce you to a series of case studies and smaller examples. Each of these scenarios mirrors realistic workplace influencing situations. A few of the scenarios are based on real-life dynamics. In each of these instances the details of the characters, the setting of the events, and the specific details of the scenarios have been fictionalized to protect the identities of the people involved.

Following an outline of the key facts of the case study or smaller example, you will find each of the following four sections.

The opportunity to influence. This section takes you behind the facts and specific detail of the action to identify the exact nature of the opportunity to influence presented in the scenario.

Handling the personalities. Here we take a deeper look at the personality of the characters with whom the main character wishes to build influence. We identify those factors that would or would not prove persuasive with that particular character's personality. This section gets behind a character's actions, words, and behaviors to understand their motivations and intentions and identify the best ways to handle them and build influence with them.

The outcome. This section describes the outcome of the main character's attempts to build influence in the scenario given their influencing style, the personality they are dealing with and the skills and tactics they employ.

Conclusions. In this last section we draw key lessons from the example.

THE NARRATIVE CASE STUDY

The final chapter of the book takes the form of a narrative case study. The narrative follows the progress of an employee who switches industry and needs to find his feet in his new job. The case study describes how the main character adjusts to the culture of his new employer over a ten-month period. It examines what influencing strategies he uses and when, how he evaluates the success of these strategies, how he builds influence with a range of colleagues, and what lessons he assimilates from making errors of judgment while trying to do so.

The narrative case study illustrates all the key learning points from the previous chapters of the book. It highlights realistic workplace influencing dynamics and explores a range of factors that the main character needs to take into account as he seeks to gain and retain influence in his new place of work.

WHAT YOU WILL NOT FIND IN THIS BOOK

This is a practical book which focuses on how to build and retain personal influence at work. It does not include discussions of organizational influencing strategies or the theoretical tactics of influence. Nor does it explicitly discuss issues of demeanor, dress sense, or body language, although it does refer to them from time to time. Instead the book focuses on which behaviors prove influential and which do not prove influential in a range of key influencing situations in your workplace.

The book mainly concerns your relationships within your workplace with your colleagues and co-workers. In other words it focuses on how to build influence with your peers, senior managers, team members and internal clients. It does not feature chapters on how to build influence with clients or customers external to your organization, although some of the techniques and ideas in the book may well provide you with ideas on how to build more influence in these relationships too. Those of you who would like a book on building and sustaining influence with your clients might like to know that one of my forthcoming books will be *Handling Clients Effectively: How to Initiate, Sustain and Retain Long-Term Customer Relationships*. The book will be published by Palgrave Macmillan.

YOUR INFLUENCING BEHAVIOR

This book is written for you, the reader, and it comes with a note of caution. In my experience, when someone tries to have influence in a certain situation at work, and finds that they either don't build much influence at all or, at some point, manage to lose the influence they had previously secured, there are usually very specific reasons for this failure. It is often because they did not think deeply enough or clearly enough about the factors that matter most to the other key players in the situation. They may have only considered some of the issues, or all of them but only from a certain perspective. Or they may have only seen things from the point of view of some of the key players or themselves and not considered all of the alternative points of view. They therefore select ineffective influencing strategies, or worse, self-defeating ones, and suffer the consequence of receiving a dent to their reputation.

My wish is that, with the help of this book, you will avoid these pitfalls more often than not and that the input from this book will enable you to:

■ Become more skilled, more effective and more productive at sizing up situations and reading them effectively before seeking to build influence in them.

■ Act in ways that will gain you the degree of influence you would like to have in the situations that matter most to you.

■ Retain and nurture the influence you do gain until you have a healthy, effective network of influential workplace relationships to draw on.

Contents

CHAPTER 1

What is Workplace Influence?

Let's begin this book by considering what the terms 'influence at work' and 'having influence in the workplace' might mean. We will define them and then examine why some people are able to acquire influence and sustain it over a period of time, why others struggle to build any influence in the first place, and why others again manage to attain a degree of influence but then subsequently lose it. We will explore the influencing dynamics in your workplace and examine what might be involved in you acquiring greater influence at work. Then we will start to look at some of the possible confusions between 'having influence' and 'having power.'

WHAT IS INFLUENCE AT WORK?

So, what does the phrase 'influence at work' conjure up for you? You might like to take a few minutes to jot down in the space below any phrases and words that come to mind when you consider the term 'influence at work':

Whatever you have written, and however much you think that having influence at work is about a person's knowledge or interpersonal attributes or simply about whom they know, you may have had difficulty describing it with any degree of certainty. You might think that 'influence at work' has an intangible quality to it and is somewhat difficult to pin down. Or you may have found that, as you considered the qualities that contribute to one or other colleague having influence in your workplace, they may not be present in the character of a third or fourth colleague whom you consider to be influential.

Influence at work is a highly individual issue. What influences one person – you, for instance – will not automatically influence another person. What influences one of your senior managers may not influence a different manager. In my work I have found that people who have acquired a degree of influence in the workplace have done so by having more than one strategy. They have a range of strategies and know which one to apply to the particular person they are dealing with in any given situation. So, is one of the main attributes possessed by a person who is perceived to have 'influence at work' the ability to select an effective strategy for influencing each specific person whose thinking they want to impact?

HAVING INFLUENCE IN THE WORKPLACE

Consider the list of words and phrases you developed to describe 'influence at work' and compare them with the points below. These points, while not intended to be an exhaustive list, outline some of the commonly cited responses. You might like to add some of your own:

- Being able to affect decisions within your areas of expertise.
- Being an opinion-former or touchstone for other people on your subject matter.
- Having the knowledge and skill to change or develop other people's perceptions.
- Knowing how to sway a discussion or decision.
- Knowing how to get the buy-in you need to take your plans forward.
- Having the ability to extend your influence beyond the area in which you could reasonably expect to hold sway given your hierarchical position.
- Being referenced at a meeting as opposed to merely attending or participating in a meeting.
- Being adroit at handling other people's agendas and working with them reasonably.
- Knowing how to say 'no' to colleagues without alienating them and thereby creating issues for yourself when you bring your next issue to the table.

- Being given the freedom and trust by your senior managers to get things done.
- Having the respect of your peers, team members and senior managers.

Perhaps the hallmark of a truly influential member of a workforce *is* that they have learned how to influence specific key people on the specific key issues over which they would like to have influence. It's not the knowledge you have on an issue that counts in and of itself, although it is certainly important, but the skill with which you apply that knowledge to the situation you want to influence. In other words it's the skill with which you use your knowledge to handle key personalities and people that will help you build influence and sustain it. It's your ability to select an effective influencing strategy for each particular colleague that will distinguish you as a skilled influencer.

HAVING INFLUENCE AT WORK: A DEFINITION

Consider the following three-part definition. Having influence at work is about:

- Introducing key information into a workplace debate which proves persuasive or decisive with your colleagues.
- Knowing how to position your interpretation of the facts, your opinions and/or your beliefs with your colleagues so that what they say or do or think is developed as a result of your input.
- Conducting yourself with passion and conveying sufficient conviction for your position that your colleagues amend, modify, alter or revise their plans, proposals or objectives as a result of considering what you say.

In other words influential people are effective at providing input to workplace discussions, be they one-to-one meetings or group forums, in a way which results in the specific colleagues they are addressing:

- Listening to their input.
- Altering their perceptions.
- Changing their position on an issue.
- Adjusting the work process they intend to use from that moment on.

Let's examine the three-part definition in the light of an example.

AN EXAMPLE OF USING INFLUENTIAL BEHAVIOR

A deputy head in a small European rural school decides to address the growing issue of playground fights and scuffles. She gathers her small group of fellow teachers together and describes the trends she has observed recently. She catalogues a number of unsavory incidents that she has witnessed in the playground during the past week, and is pleased to note that her colleagues nod their agreement at her analysis that too many children are misbehaving and picking fights with other children.

The deputy head tells her peer group that she has a proposal to put to them to address these issues. Seeing their heightened interest she outlines her proposal in clear, factual terms. She speaks clearly in a quiet voice and tells her colleagues that she has information about a successful American program that demonstrates how to turn around unruly playground behavior. It uses simple, clear rules, which are disseminated to the children. It then involves teachers in actively seeking out and praising children who follow the rules while also seeking out and reproving children who employ playground behavior which breaks the rules. The deputy head tells her colleagues that the key to making it work is that every single teacher is involved in and committed to the process.

The deputy head uses a delivery style in which she concentrates on putting across the information she wants her colleagues to consider in impartial, objective and factual terms. She uses a measured tone and speaks in a steady, simple and unfussy way. She leaves plenty of opportunity for her colleagues to ask questions and for them to debate their reaction to her proposals. However, she wants her colleagues to consider her proposals for themselves and come to their own conclusions about them. She has a strong preference that they buy in to her ideas on their own terms rather than being swayed by her belief in them. She believes that people commit when they have had sufficient time and space to consider a suggestion and form a view about it without being pressured into adopting it. While she believes very much in her plans and wants them endorsed by her colleagues she doesn't want to color their perceptions. As such, although she wants to influence them toward her view so that they endorse her plans, she decides to try to do so without conveying her personal conviction about her proposals.

The deputy head outlines the rules that form the backbone of the plan. The teachers listen to her. Some say 'That sounds good' or 'Let's try it,' but not everyone speaks. No one opposes the plan. Emboldened, the deputy head suggests that they adopt her ideas and make it a part of their regular playground duties to agree to find at least five children to praise every time they go out in the playground, as well as making a point of admonishing instances of behavior which break the rules.

However, over the following week, while a few teachers do adopt the new playground routine, many don't, and by the end of the week even those who had begun to do so have given up.

APPLYING THE DEFINITION TO THE EXAMPLE

Let's return to the three-part definition of having influence at work to see if we can account for this turn of events. Firstly, does the primary school teacher introduce key information into a workplace debate which proves persuasive or decisive with her colleagues? She certainly does, and she gets their attention. She calls a meeting and uses it to outline a growing playground situation which she sees as troubling and important. Her analysis of the issues is effective, and her colleagues recognize the situation she describes. They agree with her view that as a group they need to intervene to improve behavioral standards in the playground. They agree that the American model is simple and clear. She makes a good start to her attempt to influence her colleagues.

Secondly, does she know how to position her interpretation of the facts, her opinions and/or her beliefs with her colleagues so that what they say or do or think is developed as a result of her input? We can say that she partially does, in that some of her colleagues are influenced to say either 'That sounds good' or 'Let's try it' during the meeting, and that these colleagues do, for a time, adopt the new approach to playground duties. But some of her colleagues are left cold by her influencing style, and while they don't verbally oppose her plans or give voice to their concerns, they are not influenced either. These colleagues leave the meeting without committing to the proposals, and don't look for opportunities to issue children with reprimands or praise at break times.

Thirdly, does the deputy head conduct herself with passion and convey sufficient conviction for her position that her colleagues amend, modify, alter or revise their plans, proposals, or objectives as a result of listening to her? No, she doesn't. The deputy head deliberately keeps her own passionate belief in her proposals out of the presentation, preferring to use a composed and detached delivery style which lacks conviction. Sadly for her, with this group of people, this strategy ultimately proves ineffective. It creates the impression in the minds of some of her colleagues that she is tepid about her own proposals, even though she dearly wants them to be adopted. Her low-key delivery style creates the impression that she doesn't mind whether the proposals are adopted or not, and contributes to some of the teachers failing to take the idea on board, or indeed engage with it at the meeting.

Sadly for her, the deputy head's approach fails to build her the level of influence she might have had with this group of colleagues had she used a different approach. In order to build more influence with more of her colleagues, the deputy head needs to convey her passion and personal commitment to the plan she advocates, as well as providing the other teachers with an opportunity to think through the implications of her proposals in a calm and unemotional way. Her delivery style is too understated for some of her colleagues, and although some of them are persuaded by her, others do not commit. They cannot be sure that the deputy head really means it when she says she wants the plan to work. They doubt her commitment and don't commit to it themselves. The deputy head fails to capitalize on the opportunity to influence that she has successfully created because she doesn't convey her wholehearted belief in what she is proposing.

YOUR EXPERIENCE OF 'HAVING INFLUENCE'

This example demonstrates a range of influencing factors which need to be taken into account when seeking to have influence at work. Let's now apply its principles to your workplace. In a moment I will ask you to work through a series of questions about which factors prove influential with your colleagues. But first, let's consider the following: not every group of colleagues will necessarily be as hard to influence as the primary school teachers in the example above. In your workplace you might find that only one or two of the three parts of the definition of influence are primarily important. You may find that, in the culture that prevails in your workplace, unlike the primary school teacher, you can be influential without displaying passion, and that cool, cogent, factual arguments work best with some or most of your colleagues. Or you might find that personal passion and conviction are pivotal all the time, and that these factors are more important than the timely introduction of key information. They key point is that you need to make an accurate assessment about what factors prove influential in your workplace with your particular colleagues so that you can replicate them when you need to.

I'd like you to work through the following questions in order to determine which factors prove most influential in your workplace. Step back mentally from your current or previous workplace and identify someone whom you consider to be influential. This person is likely to be a colleague to whom others listen and from whom they are willing to take counsel, someone whose opinions others solicit, and someone who contributes to the process of setting direction in the workplace.

Now you have identified someone suitable, I'd like you to identify a specific situation in which this colleague had influence. You can jot down your ideas in the space below each one:

■ Which colleague are you considering, and what is the specific situation you have brought to mind?

■ What influence did this colleague have in this specific situation?

■ What information did this colleague introduce that proved persuasive or decisive at key influencing moments?

■ How did this colleague position their interpretation of the facts, their opinions or their beliefs with colleagues? In what way did this presentation influence what other people subsequently said or did?

■ To what extent did this colleague conduct themselves with passion and convey conviction sufficient that their colleagues amended, modified, altered or revised their plans, proposals, or objectives as a result of listening to them?

Look back at what you have written. What conclusions can you come to about what factors proved influential in the situation you have been considering? You can jot down your conclusions in the space below.

ACQUIRING INFLUENCE

It is my belief that not everyone who wants to become influential in the workplace will actually manage to exert influence at work. Some people do become influential, and some people don't. Those people who do manage to acquire some degree of influence do so because they consistently behave in ways to which their colleagues respond. In other words they are adept at selecting influencing strategies and tactics that result in their colleagues more often than not amending their views and actions because of that input.

These influential people have acquired the skills and attributes that, given their particular workplace and the particular colleagues they work alongside, result in them acquiring, gaining, and retaining influence with some or all of their colleagues. There are many different ways to build influence. Some people do it through the quality of their arguments; others through their ability to inspire others to give their best; others again through careful consideration of the situation they want to address, followed by a judicious, well-crafted proposal.

Just like any other set of inter-personal skills or attributes, the art of influence needs to be worked at. The key skills need to be practiced and honed. They aren't something that some people 'have', and other people 'don't have,' like physical stature or IQ points. 'Having influence' is something that people acquire by using a skilful interpersonal approach which results in them:

- Reading the political landscape effectively.
- Assessing the opportunities to build influence.
- Selecting key opportunities to gain influence and managing them effectively.
- Consistently choosing to use behavior, strategies, and tactics that positively affect what other people think, what they do, and how they do it.
- Recognizing when to let an issue go entirely, and when to handle an issue with a light touch.

In my view 'having influence' is actually a misnomer. This term makes it sound as if the influence somehow resides within the influential person themselves, and that they call on it whenever they want to exert it. I don't think it actually works like this. I think the influence that pertains to an individual is actually an indicator of the quality of their relationships with their colleagues. No one can have influence in a vacuum, without relationships within which to be influential. So it is more true to say that 'having influence' is as much about those who wish to be influenced and listen to the person whom they see as influential as it is about those who are doing the influencing.

More properly, people 'have influence with other people' in regard to particular issues. In other words, on specific issues colleagues choose to:

- Defer to the opinion of the influential person.
- Give weight to what they say.
- Listen to them and consider their views.

Consequently colleagues choose to develop their thinking, amend their actions, and alter their work processes because of the input of the influential person. So if someone in your workplace is perceived as 'having influence,' what is really being said is that they have invested time in building influence with colleagues and co-workers, and have done so until they have got to a point where:

- They are consulted.
- Their views are respected.
- Their opinion is solicited on certain, several, or all key issues.

THREE CRITICAL QUESTIONS

Looking at it this way creates a series of critical questions:

- Why do some people find it easy to acquire influence?
- What causes some people to lose the influence they have already acquired?
- Why do some people struggle to build any influence at all?

The rest of this book will consider these questions in detail and provide answers to them. It will highlight what behavior to use to gain or retain influence in a variety of more and less challenging situations, and will examine the pitfalls of giving too little attention to certain key factors or personalities. However, at this early stage in Chapter 1, let's examine each of the questions in turn, starting with the first question.

QUESTION ONE: WHY DO SOME PEOPLE FIND IT EASY TO ACQUIRE INFLUENCE?

Although it may not look like it, I think that those people who appear to be naturally influential have worked hard to learn to use influential behavior. They have learned what behavior to use when, with whom, and in what way. Skilled influencers may come across as if they have been innately influential all their lives. But in my work I have found that being influential is a learned skill. People who have learned the skill realize that they need to build high-quality relationships with their colleagues and co-workers, especially with those who are already influential in their organization or who play a key role within it. They make it their business to establish and maintain productive working relationships with their key co-workers, and keep working at improving the quality of these relationships until they are satisfied that they have the degree of influence with them that they want over the issues that matter most to them.

This does not mean that they sit down and write out a plan for how to gain and retain influence with each one of these people, although they might do so sometimes. But it does mean that they regularly review their approach to managing those relationships, and amend it so that they consistently use behavior which will gain them influence with those with whom they wish to connect. However, having influence carries with it the risk of losing that influence. How? By:

- Making an error of judgment.
- Mishandling key issues or personalities.
- Giving insufficient weight to certain key pieces of information.

Any of these scenarios could result in a person who has acquired influence losing some or all of it, and therefore some or all of the credibility that goes with it, either with key individual colleagues or with whole groups of colleagues.

It takes effort to remain influential. It involves regularly reviewing what matters to each of the people with whom you wish to have influence, and making a mental note about how your approach to an issue they care about will impact them. It means regularly reviewing how you:

- Communicate with your key colleagues.
- Interact with them.
- Involve them in your decisions and work processes.
- Disseminate information to them.
- Make use of their time.

Basically, if you want to become an influential member of your workplace you need to be seen to work effectively with others on a consistent basis. You need to use behavior which will build your profile, earn you opportunities to talk with your colleagues about improving the quality of the work you do together, and which will create opportunities for you to work with your co-workers to enhance your joint offer to your customers. There are ways to achieve these outcomes, and the rest of the book focuses on identifying the key behaviors you need to use.

QUESTION TWO: WHAT CAUSES SOME PEOPLE TO LOSE THE INFLUENCE THEY HAVE ALREADY ACQUIRED?

Having worked hard to build influence, some people can take a wrong turn and lose the political currency that they previously attained. Some falls from grace are sudden and quite dramatic, others are slow and unremarkable. But in either case I think that the antecedent factors involve either an error of judgment or an omission on the part of the person who ultimately loses influence.

The most common pitfall that people fall into when they lose hard-won influence is that they mismanage the perception they create in the minds of key workplace colleagues, colleagues who then begin to perceive them in a less favorable light. This could happen for a number of reasons. For instance, the person who loses influence could have:

- Failed to take note of the changing political context within which they are working and misjudged when or with whom to seek influence.
- Overlooked the importance of a key personality or a key persuasive factor when handling a sensitive or high-profile issue.
- Failed to invest heavily enough in building influence with colleagues who have widely differing views or values from their own, and thereby failed to understand what matters to them in that situation.
- Decided that the influence and reputation that they have already built will be sufficient to carry them through in the future, without realizing that they need to keep working to nurture and develop that influence from one key issue to the next.

Again, this list is not meant to be exhaustive, and there will be other individual factors that account for specific instances of people who have worked to gain influence finding that they suddenly or gradually lose it. You might like to pause for a minute and identify a situation you have knowledge of where someone with influence, be it you or a colleague, lost that influence. Consider what factors caused them to lose influence and jot them down in the space below:

QUESTION THREE: WHY DO SOME PEOPLE STRUGGLE TO BUILD ANY INFLUENCE AT ALL?

I think that those people who want to become influential but who fail to acquire much or any influence at all often fall into a specific, common trap. The trap is that of confusing 'having power' with 'having influence.' Either the person thinks that having organizational status is the same as having influence, or they think that behaving in an authoritarian way will bring them true influence. In both cases they are mistaken. We will re-visit this important issue in Chapter 2 but for now let's set the scene by examining the difference between:

■ Wanting to have influence with colleagues.

And:

■ Wanting to have power over colleagues.

Let's explore this difference by examining the role of a manager, a role that you will be familiar with either from your own experience of managing people or from your experience of being managed by someone else.

It is true that most managers have a degree of organizational authority – or power – at work. It goes with the role. It is also true that most managers therefore have the potential to exert significant influence at work over the people and issues that they are in charge of. Their role provides them with the scope to do just that. If they want to, they can make changes to their part of the organization. For instance, they could decide that they want their team to work in a different way, adopting different values and work processes. They could simply issue a directive telling their people what to do differently, without working to win over to their way of thinking the people whom they wish to carry out the new working practices. While it would be much wiser to engage with their staff in an influencing process and discuss their plans and proposals with them openly and straightforwardly, some managers do handle things in this more authoritarian way.

These managers think that their role itself, and what they see as the power or kudos that attaches to it, are enough to justify them taking a directive approach and simply ordering their staff, however politely or non-aggressively they do it, to adopt the new ways of working. They therefore behave autocratically, issuing instructions and giving orders. The problem is that using authoritarian and directive behavior is not the hallmark of someone who has earned the kind of influence that I am advocating here, the kind of influence that brings with it the respect and commitment of colleagues and co-workers. Why not? Because the authoritarian attitudes and behaviors I have just described are primarily about 'having power over people' and not really about 'having influence with colleagues' at all. That is not to say that there aren't times when it would be quite appropriate for a manager to order their people to take specific actions. There may well be. But as a usual, day-to-day style of handling people and issues, adopting an autocratic style tends to limit the influence that a manager could have with their staff, not maximize it.

True Influence

Simply having a position of authority such as that of manager does not automatically give the incumbent influence as I define it here. True influence does not come from a title or a set of responsibilities, no matter how senior those responsibilities might be. Getting things done through others because your co-workers are scared not to comply with your wishes is quite different from getting things done through others because people choose to be influenced by you and want to work with you.

True influence comes from the way a manager or any member of the workforce behaves with their colleagues. It comes from the way in which they carry out their role day in, day out, and the way in which they engage with the people around them. This description doesn't imply that they have to get on with, agree with, and be pleasant to their colleagues all the time. Far from it. Truly influential people say what they think, argue their point, disagree sometimes passionately with their colleagues, and depending on the issues they want to address, can become unpopular and even be disliked for periods of time. But they continue to handle themselves and others with respect, even when they decide that their will must prevail on certain key issues.

The Dangers of Confusing 'Having Power' with 'Having Influence'

The issue for someone who confuses 'having power' with 'having influence' is that while their behavior may find favor with people who want to be directed or who respond well to authoritarian management styles, others may not respect it and may regard it as not being influential at all. They may think that the behavior they observe doesn't promote and foster high-quality relationships and is only self-serving. They may think that instead of being focused on building collaborative or at least effective workplace relationships, the behavior they observe is primarily about doing what is comfortable or expedient for the person in authority. They may think that instead of helping others to produce high-quality work processes, the behavior they observe is mainly about the senior person retaining control of decision-making or problem-solving processes because it is comfortable for them to work that way.

These outcomes do not result in the manager in question building influential links with their colleagues. Rather, over time, they result in this person injuring their relationships and:

- Becoming isolated from colleagues.
- Being omitted from information-giving loops.
- Being excluded from decision-making and problem-solving forums.
- Becoming unable to obtain new ideas, commitment or ownership from their team members.

It can be the case that someone who concentrates on seeking to have control or power over people rather than on seeking to build influence with them can end up boxing themselves into a corner, and can, in real terms, find that they end up without any or much true influence at all.

SUMMARY AND NEXT CHAPTER

This chapter has focused on setting the scene for the rest of the book. It has:

- Presented a three-part definition of influential behavior.
- Suggested that in different workplaces different aspects of the definition will be more or less important.
- Encouraged you to think through what 'having influence' means in your current or previous workplace.
- Identified why some people appear to gain influence easily and without much apparent effort.
- Explored some of the main reasons why some people might lose the influence they have previously worked hard to build.
- Discussed some of the reasons why some people might struggle to build any influence at all.
- Started the process of examining the difference between 'having influence with colleagues' and 'having power over people.'

The following chapter will explore in detail the links, interconnections and differences between building greater influence, acquiring greater responsibility, and having greater power at work.

CHAPTER 2

Influence, Power, and Responsibility

You are working to attain greater influence at work. You find that with greater influence comes added responsibility and the potential to exert greater power in the workplace. How do you handle the three inter-connected issues of influence, responsibility, and power so that you keep your duty toward your employing organization firmly at the forefront of your mind?

These three separate but inter-connected issues are the subject of this chapter. The chapter will explore some of the key differences between wanting to build influence to help your part of the organization better achieve its aims and objectives, and wanting to acquire power over others simply for the sake of being able to exercise it. It will highlight the key attitudinal differences and the key differences in objectives between those of you who:

- Wish to build and sustain greater influence with your colleagues so that you can make a more significant contribution to your organization's development.
- See building greater influence as a way of acquiring greater organizational status so that you can enjoy the benefits such a position will afford you.

The chapter will examine why this distinction matters, what might motivate you to want more power at work, and what the consequences might be for you if you knowingly or unknowingly step over the line and use your position of influence to work in ways that might be comfortable for you but that are not in the best interests of the organization that employs you. The chapter will help you to decide for yourself what it is you really mean when you claim that you would like to 'have greater influence at work.'

It will therefore focus on you and your inner motivation. It will help you to assess:

■ What you hope to gain by building greater influence at work.
■ Your attitude to having the greater responsibility that necessarily attaches to having greater influence.
■ Your understanding of the connection between 'having greater influence' and 'having greater power.'

INFLUENCE AND RESPONSIBILITY

Having greater influence with your colleagues brings with it the opportunity to:

■ Affect their decisions.
■ Create change.
■ Input to problem-solving processes.
■ Encourage colleagues to adopt different or amended goals.
■ Motivate colleagues toward handling their workplace processes and relationships according to new and different values. These values may well reflect your own preferences. They could include, for instance, displaying a greater degree of attention to detail or demonstrating greater regard for the welfare of staff. They might also reflect your desire to set more ambitious targets or to reorganize your organization's service delivery so that it is more clearly in line with what customers want.

In this sense 'having greater influence' brings with it the opportunity to have a greater say in how things are done in your workplace. Basically, having greater influence enables you to play a role in defining how your part of the organization achieves its goals and objectives. It means that you gain the opportunity to participate more fully in the life of the organization in which you work, and can play a more direct role in shaping how that organization goes about its work. But having greater influence also brings with it a very real responsibility: the responsibility to handle effectively the room for maneuver that your new-found influence will inevitably bring you. Consider the following example.

CASE STUDY ONE: INTERIM MANAGER

The owner of a small web-based company that matches coaches to potential clients decides that he wants to give one of his four employees more responsibility in the office. He is concerned that the firm has seen a reduction in revenue and repeat orders from coaches wanting to take advantage of the opportunity to advertise on his company's website. He decides that he will place one of his four employees, a woman in her early 30s, in charge of the other three employees as interim manager so that he can devote himself to selling and marketing his business to the large organizations that purchase services from the coaches who advertise with him. He plans to be out of the office for up to a week at a time for most of the next two months meeting existing and potential clients.

The woman he wants to promote currently handles the national database that is so crucial to his business. She has been with the company for three years and is well liked by the other three members of his workforce. The owner of the business thinks that she is keen to learn and ready to make the step up to a managerial role. He forms the view that she wants to make a fuller contribution to the life of the company. He feels sure that she will be able to step up from peer to manager, and will be well placed to handle her three existing colleagues with sufficient aplomb and skill that they and she will still be able to work well together under the new reporting structure. He calls her into his office and tells her his plans.

Initially thrilled to be singled out for promotion, the national database manager quickly brings herself back down to earth. She tells her boss that she would like to go away, think through the implications of what she has been discussing with him, and return at the end of the day to his office to talk further.

During the rest of the day the national database manager mulls over what she has been asked to do and develops a list of issues for discussion with her boss. At 4.30 she returns to his office.

There are a number of ways in which the national database manager could handle the meeting with her boss. Let's explore three of them:

■ She tells her boss that she is really pleased to have his confidence and would like to take the role. But she also tells him that she has a number of concerns about how her colleagues might react to her being given greater influence in the office. She tells him that in her opinion true influence comes from establishing liking and respect among her co-workers. She says that she is concerned that, in such a small team, she will need to make sure that she treads carefully. She points out that some members of staff might not like her being promoted above their heads, and may wonder what qualities or characteristics she possesses that they apparently don't possess. She tells her boss that she is looking forward to the challenge of managing the office in his absence and is conscious of the need to tread sensitively but firmly. She ends the meeting by saying that her goal in his absence will be to work with her ex-peer group to identify and implement a series of performance improvements that will increase the quality of service the company offers to its customers.

■ She tells her boss that she is really pleased to be asked to manage the office and would like to accept the role. She says that she is greatly looking forward to working more closely with him on a day-to-day basis. She says that although she realizes that he will be out of the office for much of the following two months, she expects that he and she will be in close contact during that time, and she is looking forward to holding the fort for him in his absence. She says that, should he be happy with her work over the next two months, she would like him to consider her for a pay rise at the end of that period.

■ She tells her boss that she won't let him down and that, as she will be working on his behalf in his absence and in his stead for the two months of his travel commitments, she thinks it would work best if she moved into his office while he is out visiting clients.

The Opportunity to Influence

In this scenario the database manager has an opportunity to prove to her boss that she is worthy of the increased responsibility he wishes to give her, and of the faith he is showing in her by promoting her. However, if she accepts the new role she will need to influence more than her boss that she is up to the task. She will also need to influence her erstwhile peers that she can still work productively with them, albeit in a more senior role, and that the promotion she has been given is one she merits. Her challenge will be to convince her ex-peer group that she deserves the promotion above them and will still be an effective and able co-worker to them, albeit one with more seniority and influence than before. If she fails to accomplish these things effectively she may lose the liking and respect she has earned from her colleagues, and the faith of her boss, who is placing considerable trust with her.

Handling the Personalities

Let's explore the three instances to examine how the national database manager regards the opportunity that is being offered to her.

The First Instance

In the first instance the national database manager focuses the afternoon meeting with her boss around her understanding of the complexity of the task before her. She characterizes herself as someone fully aware of the trust and influence he wants to place with her, and outlines her understanding of the challenges and potential pitfalls for her of accepting the role. She tells him that the move she is being asked to make, while one she wholeheartedly wants, is also one that needs careful handling. She tells him that she recognizes that she needs to handle her ex-peers sensitively and adroitly if she is to retain their good regard and maintain the influential, effective working relationships she currently has with them. She makes it clear to her boss that she sees her promotion as a sign of his good faith in her, and that she is motivated to repay that good faith by making sure that she uses her role to improve the standard of the team's work without upsetting her colleagues in the office.

The Second Instance

In the second instance the national database manager focuses her afternoon meeting on her relationship with her manager. She only speaks to him about her wish to keep regularly in touch with him, and describes her role as one in which she will 'hold the fort' for him. She fails to mention her responsibility to use her new influence wisely around the office, and doesn't appear to realize that she needs to tread carefully if she is to maintain the trust and goodwill of her erstwhile peers. She characterizes herself as someone who will be looking to her boss for a lead, and describes her new role as primarily being about maintaining closer contact with him. She doesn't seem to notice that the role is primarily about her managing the office effectively in his absence.

Her boss could be forgiven for wondering if she sees her new promotion simply as an opportunity to take a lead from him rather than fully shoulder the responsibility he wants to give to her. He could also be forgiven for wondering whether she has failed to consider any of the political sensitivities involved in managing her former peers. He may think that the national database manager has misunderstood the challenge before her, and only sees it as a hierarchical advancement rather than an opportunity to use that advancement to influence her colleagues. He may even wonder if he has made a sound decision in selecting her for promotion. Indeed, when she puts in her request for a pay rise, having failed to articulate any understanding of the true task before her, he might start to wonder if he shouldn't change his mind. Of course none of these things prove conclusively that she will prove a poor choice for the role. But they do point to the possibility that she might be ill-equipped to carry the role off well.

The Third Instance

In the third instance the boss can have no doubt at all that he has misjudged the character of his national database manager. On returning to his office that afternoon she only speaks with him about moving into his office in his absence. This demonstrates that she feels out of her depth inter-personally, sees her new role as being about the increased status it affords her, and wants to have an office separate from her colleagues because it will place her at a comfortable distance from the colleagues she is now charged with managing. These are clear signals of her discomfort at the inter-personal challenge of managing her ex-peers, while being equally clear signals that she is more than comfortable with the increased status her role will afford her. She doesn't talk at all about her responsibility to use her increased influence well. She doesn't mention the political sensitivity of managing ex-peers, nor does she demonstrate any understanding of the fact that having greater responsibility means that she needs the people-handling, influencing and political management skills to go with the title and the manager's office.

The Outcome

In the first instance the boss can feel pleased with himself that he appears to have made a sound judgment by placing greater responsibility into the hands of someone who apparently understands the challenges before her. Whether she will have an equally clear grasp on how to behave to discharge her responsibility effectively is yet to be proven, but the signs are good. He will need to keep an eye on her and be prepared to offer her coaching and counsel should she find making the transition more rather than less problematic, but the early prognosis is that she is well placed to make an able interim manager in his absence.

In the second instance the boss ought to be a little concerned. His national database manager has only understood half of the story: the part that is about her own self-advancement. She doesn't seem to have understood that taking the new role means that she will need to maintain liking and respect with her colleagues *through the quality of her behavior with them*. She thinks that they will bestow liking and respect on her because of her position. It doesn't occur to her that she cannot simply assume that the good relationships she currently enjoys with her colleagues will automatically be maintained in her new role should she start to use a different approach, one characterized by a heightened sense of her own status. And given the way she is talking, this is a distinct possibility. Her boss could be forgiven for starting to think twice about going through with his plans to promote her.

In the third instance the boss needs to consider seriously putting a halt to his plans to promote the national database manager, and deciding instead to handle the issues before him in a different way. The opportunity to have greater influence has clouded her judgment, and she cannot see the difference between managing the office well in his absence and her own increased status. She sees her new role in terms of where she will sit in the office, what status she will have, and how she will therefore feel about her new role. She doesn't see past herself sufficiently to consider what she is there to do along with the other people in the office: work to make the business more profitable. With this mindset she may well mishandle her new-found influence in the office, alienate her colleagues, and jeopardize the quality of the work the firm is doing at a time when its books don't look good.

Conclusions

The case study demonstrates that a person's attitude to having increased influence and responsibility is very often one that only comes to light once they have been promoted. It is often only at the moment of being offered increased influence that people recognize what it means to them. And even then very few people can put it into words. It shows instead in what they talk about when they discuss their new role, how they conduct themselves in advance of being promoted into it, and what they say will be their priorities in the role once they assume it. In this case study the database manager adopts three distinctly different approaches to the prospect of promotion, and in only one of these instances could the business owner proceed, confident that his newly promoted employee is likely to turn out well.

We have taken an initial look at the potential for confusion in the mind of an employee who is offered promotion. Let's now explore the links between having greater influence and having greater power in more detail and apply the material to your own working life. We'll start with you.

WHAT DO YOU WANT?

Presumably if you have read this far you must want to acquire greater influence at work, or at the very least, you want to understand what might be involved in gaining greater influence. However, I do want to ask you to look inwards and clarify for yourself what it is about 'having greater influence' that attracts you. Consider the following questions. You can jot down your answer to each of the questions in the space below it:

■   What does having greater influence at work mean to you in your work?

■   Why do you want greater influence?

■   What do you think might be the downsides of having greater influence for you in your workplace?

■ What attracts you about having the greater responsibility which will inevitably accompany any increased influence you acquire?

■ What scares you about having greater responsibility?

THE REALITY OF HAVING GREATER INFLUENCE

You might like to review what you have written and compare it with the following ideas. For many of you having greater influence at work may be synonymous in your minds with having greater autonomy and more freedom to get done the things you want to do in the way you want to do them. However, I am unconvinced that this is true. Greater autonomy and independence pertain to self-employed people, not to members of organizations. By its very nature organizational life requires that you learn to work effectively with a range of people with whom you may have little in common. Those of you working in an organization will need to get the buy-in of colleagues before you can act if you are to launch a new initiative, design and sell a new service or conduct a piece of research with customers, for instance. So for people in organizations, I think that having greater influence at work means working hard to convince colleagues that your:

■ Ideas are worth considering.
■ Input is worth soliciting.
■ Opinions are worth listening to.

But having greater influence will not automatically bring you greater autonomy or more freedom. It will give you the opportunity to convince your colleagues that there is something in what you say, and that your input will enhance the process and quality of the work. But that isn't quite the same as saying that having greater influence at work will bring you more breathing space. It isn't likely to. In fact it may mean that more people seek you out, more people rely on your input, more people want to talk to you, and more people want your energy. Your time may become more stretched and your head more full of issues and items that others put to you for your consideration. You may need to become better at managing your 'to do list,' sharper at prioritizing your tasks, and smarter at getting to the nub of the matter both in what you say and in how you question and converse with colleagues. In other words your area of influence may expand, but so will your area of responsibility.

The Benefits of Having Greater Influence

So, why would you want greater influence? I think the benefit of having greater influence is that it enables you to provide input to the evolving agenda of your organization. It enables you to play a part in determining what:

- Goals and objectives the organization of which you are a part will set and strive for.
- Values and ethical principles it will work by.
- Standards of service it will seek to provide its customers with.

Truly influential people use their influence to improve the standard of service their team or organization offers to its customers, and seek to develop and support their staff in line with their role goals and objectives. Truly influential people use their influence to benefit their *organization* not *themselves*. Sure, they may enjoy financial and prestige benefits as a result of being influential, effective, and successful. But they keep their minds firmly on the fact that they are there to make sure that the organization of which they are a part succeeds, reaches its objectives, supports its staff, and serves its customers well. They are also mindful of the responsibility that goes with their position of influence, and recognize that other people inevitably are affected by the decisions they make and the behavior they use while they are at work.

The Downsides of Having Greater Influence

So what are the downsides of having greater influence? They are individual to you, and really only you can say. Maybe you don't want to face the fact that, should you acquire greater organizational influence, you might have to provide input to decisions that affect other people's working lives. Maybe you'd be discomfited by the reality that, should other people listen to you and be swayed by proposals that subsequently prove unsuccessful or ineffective, you would have to shoulder some of the fault. Maybe you'd be unnerved by the likelihood that a more senior and influential position will likely involve you to a greater degree in political considerations or the unpalatable side of organizational life, such as having to decide who will be made redundant or who will take a pay cut. So, you might like to jot down your answer to the following question in the space below it:

■ To what extent do the benefits of having greater influence outweigh the risks and downsides as far as you are concerned?

USING YOUR INFLUENCE UNWISELY

So far we have been considering the upside and the downside of acquiring greater organizational influence. Let's now take a sideways step and focus for a few minutes on a related issue: that of using one's position of influence to make decisions that are self-serving. Consider the following short examples:

■ The business owner who asks one of his staff members to come in early and open up the office so that he can relinquish the task, have an extra half hour's sleep each morning, and arrive later. His staff members start to question his commitment to the business.

■ The sales manager who alters the bonus system so that she can pay herself a proportion of her team's earnings as well as a percentage of her own actual sales revenue. Her team members feel resentful and trust her less.

■ The school governor who uses his influence to ensure that his own family member jumps the queue and gets a place at a sought-after school before those on the waiting list. His peers question his judgment and wait for his next mistake.

In each of these situations the main character starts to use their position to make decisions on the basis of what is easier or more beneficial for them or their family members, rather than on the basis of what is right for their organization, its staff, or the users of the services they manage. Clearly the incentives and the reasons behind the three instances are very different in quality and nature. But the opportunities for managers to act in this way are numerous, and only you will be able to decide where you personally would draw the line, and under what circumstances you would decide to cross that line.

Each of these characters has been tempted into the trap of using their position to prioritize their own wish to have a few more hours sleep a week, or to take home more money, or to gain a school place for their family member above all other considerations. The fallacy here is that there will be no uncomfortable consequences for them to deal with as a result of making this decision. This isn't true, and the final sentence in each short example attests to this fact.

Retaining Power and Control

Creating a way of working where decisions, and therefore power, are retained by you alone, or are retained in the hands of a few people including you, causes those without influence to feel to varying degrees:

■ Bored, underutilized, and stagnant.
■ Undervalued and unchallenged.
■ Uninvolved, uncommitted, and unwilling to take responsibility.
■ Angry and resentful at what they see as a misuse of power.

Under these circumstances, people react differently. Some people place their commitment and energy elsewhere, usually into their private lives. Others do just enough at work but no more. Others again get their own back on the manager involved by operating below par. They can fail to own problems that properly sit with them, and often feel cynical toward those above them who, as they see it, misuse their role and take advantage of their position of influence.

As a way of managing people, retaining power and control doesn't work, and often causes a catalogue of problems which managers and leaders subsequently complain about while failing to realize that their own conduct has inspired all of them. A far better way forward is to build genuine influence with your colleagues by working with them in an open, collaborative, and skilled way. Subsequent chapters of this book will take you through a series of tools to help you achieve this aim.

USING YOUR INFLUENCE WISELY

So if you are to avoid the pitfalls of using your position to meet your own needs *and* you are to avoid the pitfalls of confusing increased responsibility or influence with increased power, what do you need to keep in mind? You might like to ask yourself to what extent you actively and consistently use whatever influence you have available to you to:

- Redefine your organization's goals in line with its customer requirements.
- Listen to customer-facing staff.
- Improve work processes.
- Reward top performers.
- Incentivize innovative staff.
- Actively support your employees.
- Provide your team with the ongoing training and tools they need to handle their roles effectively.

Those of you who use your influence to attend to these things but do so infrequently and with insufficient passion may need to reassess your use of your time. You could ask yourselves what else you could be doing to enable the part of the organization over which you have influence to become more effective. Those of you who don't do these things very much at all, or ever, may need to ask yourselves what value you add to your organization by focusing on priorities other than those listed above.

YOUR RESPONSE

So the questions for you to consider are these. In seeking to acquire greater influence at work, to what extent are you:

- Attracted by the opportunity to make a genuine contribution to the organization that employs you, helping it improve its work processes and redefine its goals in tandem with a range of your colleagues?
- Attracted by the potential for increased kudos, increased organizational authority, and increased organizational status so that you can retain power for yourself?

These are hard questions to ask yourself, and you may not know the answers straight away. But they are important questions to answer. You can jot down whatever ideas come to you in the space below.

This chapter has touched on the complex and interrelated issues of influence, responsibility, and power at work. These are issues that have subtle but powerful dynamics at the heart of them. Those of you who would like to explore in more detail the links between having greater responsibility and acquiring increased organizational authority, and the links between power and status at work, might want to refer to Chapters 6–9 of *Managing Politics at Work: The Essential Toolkit for Identifying and Handling Political Behaviour in the Workplace* (by Aryanne Oade, and published by Palgrave Macmillan in 2009). In Chapters 6–9 I discuss the issues involved in working alongside colleagues to get things done, and examine the links between politics, power, and influence at work.

SUMMARY AND NEXT CHAPTER

This chapter has focused on the three inter-connected issues of attaining increased influence, having greater responsibility, and using the power available to you in your role wisely or unwisely. The chapter suggested that:

- Some people confuse having greater influence with having greater power.
- Often people might not know what their true attitude to having increased influence and greater responsibility is until they are confronted with the reality of a new and more senior role.
- Those people who think that the main focus of a promotion is their own status miss the point.
- The mark of a truly influential person is that their objective remains steadfastly that of improving the quality of the part of the organization over which they have influence, and they put this aim above all other considerations.

The rest of the book focuses on the key skills and tools you need to build influence with a range of colleagues and co-workers. The following chapter will take an in-depth look at the different values and styles people use at work. We explore how a clear understanding of these differences can enable you to build influence with key people even when the opportunities to meet and talk to existing opinion formers can be short and pressured.

CHAPTER 3

Four Sets of Influencing Values

One of the starting points for influencing other people effectively is to know your own influencing style first: *your* values, *your* strengths, *your* areas for development, and *your* characteristics as an influencer. The more you know about how you naturally seek to influence others, the better placed you'll be to make an objective assessment about what different or similar factors are most likely to prove persuasive with the specific people you want to influence. The more you understand about what influences you, the more effective you will be at selecting influencing strategies and arguments with your colleagues' preferences and needs in mind. The more clued up you are about what proves influential with you, the more likely you will be to make valid distinctions between:

■ What you need to hear to be influenced

And

■ What the colleagues you want to influence need to hear to be influenced.

They may not be the same. Many people fail to acquire influence with key colleagues because they assume that what influences those colleagues automatically corresponds with what influences them. They fail to build the influence they want to have because they don't select influencing arguments that prove persuasive with their *audience*.

This chapter will therefore focus on you and your influencing style. It will help you to step back from your day-to-day work and:

■ Identify the values behind your natural approach to influencing.
■ Highlight the benefits, pitfalls, and characteristics of your natural influencing style or styles.
■ Develop your self-awareness and self-knowledge so that you become better placed to make an objective assessment about the situation in which you want to have influence.

- Illustrate how to tailor your influencing conversations around the values of the colleagues with whom you are speaking.
- Highlight the reputational risks of failing to consider your colleagues' values as well as your own when you engage them in an influencing conversation.

INFLUENCING YOUR COLLEAGUES

Let's start with you. Specifically, let's begin by equipping you with the knowledge and tools you need to make an accurate assessment about the values behind your approach to influencing. This is important knowledge to have because it will make explicit the factors that matter most to you in any situation, and it will provide a basis from which to clarify what different concerns, needs, and aims your colleagues may have as you seek to build influence with them.

The key point is that while you may be convinced about the merits of your case, your colleagues might not be, no matter how factual your analysis or effective your presentation of the factors involved. Just because you place weight on a particular set of factors – for instance, potential upcoming unmanaged risks that you perceive, or potential opportunities that you think are being overlooked, or the impact of a poorly thought-out decision on the people who will be affected by it – doesn't mean that your colleagues will be as concerned with these factors as you are. Just because you are convinced that the issues and values that matter most to you are pre-eminent concerns doesn't mean that your colleagues will agree with you, or be open to being influenced by your argument.

They might see the same situation from a completely different perspective from yours, or might place less weight upon the facts and issues that you think are persuasive. The more you continue to talk about your concerns and the factors that seem decisive to you *without acknowledging and addressing the different issues that matter to them,* the more you are liable to lose their interest and fail to influence their view of the situation. An accurate understanding of what matters most to your key colleagues, of what influences *them* and of how that differs from what influences you, is vital if you are to build influence with them.

FOUR SETS OF INFLUENCING VALUES

So let's start by identifying the values that underpin your characteristic work style, before identifying some of the key features of your natural influencing style. Below are descriptions of four different sets of workplace values, values that underpin four different work styles. You might naturally use:

■ Only one of the sets of values in every situation you encounter at work. In this case you have a well-established preference for these values in comparison with any of the other ways of doing things.

■ A combination of two or three of the sets of values simultaneously. In this case your preference is to satisfy two or three potentially contradictory sets of values at any one time.

■ All four styles simultaneously. In this case you set yourself the challenge of adopting an approach in which you seek to address four different sets of values simultaneously.

■ Different styles with different groups of colleagues. In this case you might use one combination of the values with managers more senior to you, a different combination of values with your clients, and a different combination of values again with your peers or team members.

The following principles are derived from behavioral styles theories which suggest that different people will react to the same situation differently depending on their values. We will examine these values only to the extent that they are relevant to influencing. Those of you who would like to explore these issues in greater depth will find suggestions for further reading in the References and Recommended Reading at the back of the book.

As you read through the descriptions of the values that follow, remember that each of you has a unique style, and there are no rights or wrongs about values preferences. When you consider your usual workplace behaviors, which of the following four sets of values, or which combination of the four sets of values, do you most identify with?

Generating Momentum, Directing Events

Those of you who identify with this set of values may well find that you:

■ Prefer to take immediate, direct charge of events at work.
■ Use a goal-oriented and logical approach.

- Are highly motivated to seize opportunities and take advantage of openings.
- Want to understand the big picture concept behind an idea or proposal before moving on to discuss its relevance to your work.
- Like to generate momentum in a discussion or when working on a project.
- Are adept at introducing structure to facilitate progress against your goals.
- Use conversations or meetings to clarify the direction you would like to see projects and workplace events proceed in.
- Tend to give and receive information in bullet points and headlines, speaking in a rapid and punchy manner.
- Enjoy and need challenge in your work.
- Take a strategic view, and speak first about outcomes and future-oriented plans.
- Expect to be rewarded for reaching your targets.
- Get frustrated if you perceive that other people are preventing you from taking direct control over the factors you think are critical to the success of your work.
- Get frustrated if you think other people are getting in your way or slowing you down.
- Could be seen as impulsive, someone who doesn't plan sufficiently well and who is reluctant to think through the details.
- Could also be seen as someone who disregards the practical risks and pragmatic issues in favor of plunging ahead.

When seeking to build influence with colleagues you are likely to emphasize the facts, the positive benefits and outcomes that will be attained by implementing your proposals, as well as the competitive advantage that will result from adopting your suggestions. You are likely to create compelling, focused arguments which demonstrate how productivity and efficiency will be enhanced by your propositions.

Ensuring Quality, Managing Risk

Those of you who identify with this set of values may well find that you:

- Are goal-oriented and logical in your approach to situations at work.

- Are primarily interested in ensuring high-quality outputs.
- Make it a priority to identify and manage potential areas of risk in your work.
- Prefer to work within a clear structure.
- Like to monitor and evaluate progress as a way of keeping on top of your work.
- Create and use plans whenever possible to enable you to monitor progress and evaluate outcomes effectively.
- Prefer factual, data-centered arguments and discussions.
- Naturally clarify the fact of the matter and supply data to support your case.
- Provide background and rationale for your plans, including detailed supporting data and facts.
- Make a point of asking what can be learned from previous work that could prevent errors going forward.
- Prefer to consider facts and data in advance of making a decision or contributing to a meeting.
- Get frustrated if you are expected to move ahead without having had sufficient time to consider a situation fully.
- Get frustrated if you have to make a decision without having sufficient data to do so effectively.
- Get concerned if you think your understanding of a situation is insufficiently thorough to enable you to act with confidence.
- Could be seen as someone who gets bogged down in the details and who plans too much when action is needed.
- Could be characterized as someone who generates obstacles and slows projects down unnecessarily.

When seeking to build influence with colleagues you are likely to emphasize how your plans will promote high-quality, error-free work. You create factual, logical arguments which prove your case and which are usually delivered in an impartial, objective and goal-oriented manner.

Building Rapport, Contributing Excellence

Those of you who identify with this set of values may well find that you:

- Prefer to adopt the role of supportive mentor at work, guiding and prompting your colleagues toward excellent performance.

- Are committed to the work you undertake, and expect your colleagues and clients to be equally participative and involved.
- Enjoy building relationships with your colleagues characterized by a degree of rapport and harmony.
- Enjoy contributing to the growth and development of your colleagues or clients.
- Have high standards for interpersonal conduct, both in how you behave towards your colleagues and in how you expect to be treated at work.
- Prefer to work in open and trusting relationships, although you can contribute effectively without openness or trust.
- Like to talk through conflicts and arguments to find ways of resolving the issues involved.
- Naturally recognize the impact of decisions on the people who will be affected by them.
- Are adept at maintaining harmony in your relationships, even in situations where your ideas are contentious.
- Make it a priority to respond fully to the concerns and questions of the people with whom you are working.
- Value projects and ideas that will enhance the excellence of the work undertaken by your team or department.
- Get frustrated if you are expected to work with unsupportive colleagues or with co-workers who take advantage of your willingness to offer help and support.
- Get frustrated by co-workers who don't involve you or your team members in decisions that affect them.
- Get concerned if you think your views or work are not appreciated.
- Could be seen as someone who concedes ground too easily and finds it difficult not to give in on your own goals when under pressure.
- Could be regarded as someone who prefers to take direction rather than set it, and who expects a level of participation and involvement that others do not think necessary.

When seeking to build influence with colleagues you are likely to emphasize how your plans will promote teamwork and responsiveness to customers. You create personalized arguments which emphasize how performance will be improved and standards raised by your proposals.

Managing Perceptions, Marketing Achievements

Those of you who identify with this set of values may well find that you:

- Naturally bring colleagues and workplace contacts together to discuss ideas of mutual interest.
- See yourself as a facilitator and broker of workplace relationships.
- Enjoy using your network of influential contacts to get things done and to make things happen.
- Are skilled at managing other people's perceptions and marketing your achievements.
- Have a penchant for remaining flexible and spontaneous during a conversation or meeting.
- Are effective at presenting the same idea in different ways to different people so that it has maximum appeal to those with whom you are speaking.
- Naturally like to experiment, and enjoy using your resourcefulness to help colleagues to overcome problems and obstacles in their work.
- Like to be in the spotlight, acquiring influential workplace contacts.
- Get frustrated if you are expected to work within a highly structured environment or to tight deadlines.
- Get frustrated if your co-workers are unfriendly or critical of you.
- Get bored if your work involves significant amounts of routine activity.
- Could be seen as someone who is political and tricky to deal with.
- Could be regarded as someone who avoids responsibility when under pressure, and who loses sight of the goals toward which you are working.

When seeking to build influence with colleagues you are likely to emphasize how your plans will enhance reputations and build prestige. You create politically astute arguments and sell your proposals adroitly, positioning them cleverly to appeal to as many opinion formers as possible.

YOUR INFLUENCING BEHAVIOR

Which of the sets of values, or which combination of them, do you most identify with? You might like to jot down your answers to the following questions in the spaces below them:

■ Which of the sets of values are your preferred options at work?

■ Which of the other sets of values can you adopt even if they are not your preferred options?

■ Thinking about your preferred sets of values, which of their characteristics do you value and in what way are these characteristics useful to you in your work?

■ Thinking about your less preferred options, which of their characteristics do you value and in what situations do you shift gear and start to use them?

You now have some idea of which sets of values you favor at work, and which alternative sets of values you can call on should you need to. This information is important because knowing what values matter to you will help you to form sound judgments about what alternative or similar values matter to your colleagues. This is important information to have. These judgments can make all the difference when it comes to selecting which influencing arguments to emphasize to which colleague. Let's look at an example to help establish these principles. The following scenario is set in a busy technology department of a US financial consultancy firm.

CASE STUDY TWO: SHIFTING INFLUENCING STYLE

An experienced IT project manager wants to introduce a comprehensive suite of new software into the firm in which she works. The project manager believes that the software will enhance the performance of each of the firm's four East Coast offices, enabling its consultants to better serve their clients in a variety of ways. Each East Coast office is run by a different lead consultant, and the lead consultants all work in quite dissimilar ways to one another. They value different things and are open to being influenced by different factors.

The project manager is worried that her plans will prove unpopular with the firm's consultants even though she is convinced that the new software will bring many benefits to them and to the firm. She decides that, if she gets the go-ahead for her plans, she will set up a series of in-house workshops to help the consultants get to grips with the new software applications and programs. But first of all she has to gain the buy-in she needs to her plans from the firm's four lead consultants.

The project manager decides that she will meet with the firm's four lead consultants separately. She decides to invest time in developing four different presentations, one for each of them. As it happens she uses a mixture of the first and second sets of values, but she recognizes the need to flex her influencing style with the different values that matter to the lead consultants. She sets aside time to plan and prepare for four separate meetings, each of which she arranges in the relevant lead consultant's office. The project manager decides to handle each meeting differently based on her best understanding of each of the lead consultants' values, and her reading of what is most likely to influence them. Let's take a look at the four meeting formats she designs.

The First Lead Consultant

She regards the first lead consultant as being goal-oriented, logical, and big picture in his approach to his work. She sees him as someone who is motivated by challenge, and who uses an energetic, punchy delivery style. He has a reputation for becoming bored quite quickly and for getting impatient with detail. The lead consultant is active and brisk in his management of his office, is regarded as being 'me-centered' in his approach to his work, and often asks the question 'What can you do for me?' However, when under significant pressure he closes the door and steps back from his work. In this mode he generates plans and thinks through in some detail what needs to be accomplished and how before emerging from his office re-energized and ready to engage with his team. The project manager forms the view that he uses the first set of values around generating momentum and directing events, but also uses the second set of values around methodical structure when he needs to.

The project manager plans the meeting carefully. She starts by outlining the big-picture concept behind her plans: that she wants to install new software across the firm, software which will bring positive outcomes for the firm as well as for its customers. She includes a clear framework outlining the structure of her implementation program, and highlights a timescale within which the lead consultant will be able to see the expected positive results.

She breaks down the positive outcomes into four categories: benefits for the lead consultant, for his team, for the wider firm, and for the firm's customers.

She is careful not to include too much detail at this stage of the meeting, since she thinks this would bore the lead consultant and result in him getting impatient with her. She concentrates on the concept she wants him to buy in to, and adopts the view that he would prefer a conversation focused on the bigger picture: what she is proposing to do, what it will achieve for the firm, and what specific outcomes will benefit his business. She thinks that, having absorbed this information, should he have specific questions to put to her, he will do so.

She decides to use a punchy, sharp, solutions-focused style throughout the meeting. She thinks that she will be best placed to influence him if she makes a point of describing how the new software will help him to capitalize on new opportunities to impress customers and retain business, as well by pointing out the new options that it will create for his consultants to enhance their offer to their clients.

The Second Lead Consultant

The second lead consultant is a very different character, and the project manager develops a quite different approach to the influencing conversation she wants to hold with her. This lead consultant is quite cautious in nature, and is primarily 'data-centered' in her approach to work and workplace issues. She often asks the question 'What conclusions does the data lead to?' She has dual aims of ensuring high-quality work while identifying and managing risk. She is most comfortable dealing with factual, goal-oriented information presented in a detailed, methodical way, and is most influenced by an impartial, cool delivery style. This lead consultant emphasizes the need to monitor progress and evaluate outcomes, so the project manager forms the view that she has a clear preference for the second set of values around ensuring quality and managing risk.

The project manager decides to include a detailed step-by-step outline of her proposals in the meeting. She begins with a thorough analysis of the rationale for the implementation of the new software, before continuing with a detailed examination of the budget, timings, and work involved in each stage of the program. She breaks the program down into four phases: the purchase of the new software, the installation, the training programs for the consultants, and the post-implementation maintenance program. She wants this lead consultant to understand the ins and outs of her proposals in full so that she can consider them in the detail she needs.

She thinks that this lead consultant will want to go away and think about what she has heard during the meeting so that she can reflect on the proposals and consider their implications for her business. The project manager decides to leave a detailed written reminder of her presentation with the lead consultant so that she can reflect on the content of the meeting after they have finished speaking. The project manager thinks it unlikely that this lead consultant will want to make a decision then and there, but that she may want to come back to her after the meeting with questions or requests for more information about specific issues.

The project manager handles the meeting at a pace that allows the lead consultant to reflect on what has just been said and absorb that information before being taken through the next point. Because she is both thorough and rigorous, the project manager thinks that the lead consultant will want full answers to any points she puts to her. Being risk-averse, this lead consultant will most likely be influenced by an approach that emphasizes how the outcomes from the implementation program tie into and build on the current technology and its application to the work of the consultants. She will also want to talk through her concerns about the proposals in a calm and factual way.

The project manager thinks that her approach to the meeting needs to demonstrate how the new software will extend the quality of the consultancy team's work if it is to catch the imagination of the lead consultant. Furthermore, she has to show that she has thought through and planned to handle a range of risks and potential areas of concern for the consultant team during the installation process. As the lead consultant is primarily data-centered in her approach, the project manager wants to influence her through her own thorough knowledge of and research about the new software and its benefits for the firm.

The Third Lead Consultant

The next lead consultant is a different character again, and the project manager decides to develop a third, tailor-made meeting for him in order to maximize her chances of influencing him. The third lead consultant is primarily relationship and process oriented, is interested in individual and team development, and wants to deliver excellent work that is highly valued by his clients. He values his workplace relationships, and likes to build rapport or harmony with his colleagues and clients whenever he can. He is often interpersonally warm and is usually open, and he especially responds well to a collaborative way of doing things. He is 'you-centered' in his approach to work and workplace issues, and naturally asks himself 'How can I support you?' when working with his colleagues and clients. He is interested in finding ways to promote excellence in the work done by his team, and is often influenced by the personal conviction of a presenter for what they are saying. However, he is also very keen to make progress against his goals, and gets frustrated with delays. The project manager forms the view that he primarily uses the third set of values around building rapport and contributing excellence, and also uses the first set of values around generating momentum and achieving outcomes.

She wants the meeting to focus on his key interest: the growth, development, and performance of his staff and clients. She tells him how the new technology will add value to his team's work, enhance individual and team performance, and enable them to offer a better standard of service to their clients. She also explains to him what steps she will put in place to mitigate the disruption that the software switch will cause to his team. She emphasizes how much they will enjoy learning to use the software, and that the training programs she and her team are devising will be a stimulating and exciting opportunity for his team to learn together.

The project manager wants to handle her meeting with this lead consultant in an interactive manner. She decides to include planned opportunities for him to input to it. She is keen to demonstrate her willingness to work with him in a shared process. So she listens effectively to his points and questions, reflects back her understanding of what he has said, and asks insightful questions of him to elicit his opinion on her proposals.

The project manager thinks that this lead consultant may like time to think about her proposals before deciding whether or not to support them, so she leaves him with a written reminder of the key points. But ultimately, she thinks that he will be influenced by an approach that emphasizes her own belief in her proposals, coupled with her desire to involve him in a participative implementation program which will improve his team's ability to perform excellently. These are the key points she concentrates on getting across.

The Fourth Lead Consultant

The last lead consultant uses a different style again, and the project manager decides to redesign her meeting format a fourth time in order to give herself the best chance of influencing her. This lead consultant sees herself as an influential person. She is an able networker and facilitator of workplace relationships, being interpersonally skilled, both adroit with people and politically astute. She is 'us-centered' in her approach to work and workplace relationships, and naturally asks herself, 'What can we achieve together?' However, she has a keen eye for detail and is no fool. While she enjoys bantering with colleagues she also wants to see evidence of rigorous application. The project manager decides that she uses a mixture of the fourth set of values around managing perceptions and marketing achievements, and the second style around detailed planning.

The project manager thinks that this lead consultant is likely to make leaps of thought between the material she presents to her at the meeting and the ideas that come to her as she absorbs the information. Therefore she wants to adopt an evolutionary approach to the meeting, one where she knows where she will start and what themes she will subsequently talk about, but where she chooses the order of those themes during the course of the meeting, based on the quality of dialogue she opens up with the lead consultant.

The lead consultant is naturally comfortable with ambiguity, so she tends to leave decisions and processes open-ended, with room for maneuver. The project manager decides that she will not impose any structure on the meeting or press her colleague for an early decision about whether or not she supports her proposals. Instead she will talk through her plans with the lead consultant and then let her give an opinion when she is ready.

She decides to focus the meeting around what the new software can do for her and her team, highlighting the ways in which implementing it will give her more tools for getting things done, and more choices for how to do it. The project manager emphasizes how the new software will increase the lead consultant's options for impressing customers, raising her profile with them, enhancing her reputation with them, and enabling her to better market her team's achievements both to them and to her senior colleagues in the firm. She emphasizes that the project she is proposing will be stimulating and interesting, and will provide the lead consultant with a range of new and valuable tools.

Ultimately, the project manager thinks that this colleague will be influenced by an approach that is interpersonally stimulating, and that highlights how the new software will better enable the lead consultant to sell her team and raise her profile with her customers, her team members, and her senior colleagues.

The Opportunity to Influence

In this case study the project manager has a significant opportunity to influence four senior colleagues, each of whom is an opinion former in the firm, and who together form a powerful decision-making group within the business. If she succeeds in influencing them, or enough of them, so that her proposals are accepted and the new software is implemented, she stands to build a reputation as someone who:

- Is a proactive member of the workforce.
- Independently identifies opportunities to improve the technology base in the firm.
- Knows how to sell her ideas effectively to senior members of the business.

- Understands the pressures on the consultants in the firm, and knows how to work with their agendas and time constraints.
- Can be trusted to develop and implement effective, high-profile technology plans and proposals which will improve the firm's capacity to deliver to its customers.
- Could be consulted in future on additional ways to improve the firm's hardware and software capability.

Handling the Personalities

In order to succeed with her plans to influence each of the lead consultants to adopt her proposals, the project manager has to handle four very different personalities. She needs to demonstrate to each lead consultant that her proposals will benefit the firm, its customers, and its consultants, but she needs to do so in a way that is individually tailored for each of the four of them.

For lead consultant one she needs to adopt an influencing style that is tailored to the first set of values but also appeals to the second set. This presentation needs to:

- Be clearly goal and outcome-oriented.
- Be delivered in a punchy, factual, and logical style.
- Outline the big picture concept first before moving on.
- Follow a clear structure.
- Describe the positive outcomes and benefits of the project at the start.
- Emphasize both the challenge and the rewards of the proposals.
- Demonstrate how momentum will be generated and sustained throughout the project.
- Clearly identify how the project manager will take direct charge of the project and be personally accountable to the lead consultant.
- Leave room for more detailed information if requested.

For lead consultant two the project manager needs to adopt an influencing style that is tailored to the second set of values. This presentation needs to:

- Be clearly goal and outcome-oriented.
- Be delivered in a detailed, data-centered, and logical manner.
- Demonstrate a planned and methodical approach.

- Include rigorous detail about the background and rationale behind the proposals.
- Outline how the software will promote high-quality, meticulous work.
- Outline what risks and areas of concern the project manager has already identified, and illustrate how each one of them will be managed.
- Provide time and space for the lead consultant to reflect.
- Make clear reference to what will change and how.

For lead consultant three the project manager needs to adopt an influencing style that is tailored to the third set of values while also appealing to the first set of values. The presentation needs to:

- Be process-oriented and build rapport.
- Be characterized by an emphasis on working in a collaborative process with the lead consultant.
- Demonstrate how the proposals will enable the lead consultant's team to carry out excellent work.
- Demonstrate the ways in which the new software will help each member of the team to develop their skills and offers to the firm.
- Provide opportunities for the lead consultant to give input to the process of the meeting.
- Give the lead consultant thinking time before asking him for a decision.
- Demonstrate the project manager's belief in her own plans.
- Be delivered in an involving, warm, and engaging manner.
- Clearly demonstrate how the new software will support the lead consultant in achieving his goals.

Finally, for lead consultant four the project manager needs to adopt an influencing style that appeals to the fourth set of values while also being relevant to the second set. This presentation needs to:

- Be process-oriented and build rapport.
- Be focused around themes which can be referred to in any order.
- Demonstrate how the new software will enable the lead consultant to enhance her profile and reputation with her clients.

- Clarify how the new software will enable her to become more influential and promote herself more effectively within the firm.
- Be delivered within an open-ended, evolutionary structure.
- Provide opportunities for the lead consultant to go off at a tangent and discuss the exciting possibilities engendered by the proposals.
- Provide stimulating and novel options for her team's future development.
- Be delivered in an easy-going, relaxed and conversational style.

The Outcome

In this scenario the project manager's tailored approach to handling the four meetings serves her well. She is successful at creating enough interest in her proposals that she is given the go-ahead for a pilot scheme involving one of the four offices of the firm. Providing that both consultant and client feedback is positive, and the project manager expects that they will be, she will then be able to roll out the new technology into all four offices.

Conclusions

This case study demonstrates that influencing is a very individual issue. An approach that proves to be influential with one lead consultant will not necessarily prove to be influential with another. In selecting an approach for each person, an approach that she hopes will sway their opinion towards her plans and proposals, the project manager draws on her knowledge of each person's style. Her understanding of their preferred ways of receiving information and methods of contributing to meetings allows her to create four individual approaches to what eventually proves to be a series of very important meetings for her. She considers that the importance of the four meetings justifies the time it takes her to plan for each of them. She succeeds, and her investment of time and effort is rewarded with a pilot program and with enhanced credibility with the lead consultants.

MAKING THE MOST OF YOUR OPPORTUNITIES TO INFLUENCE

Many of the opportunities you have to build influence with your colleagues will be short and pressurized. Some of them will be unplanned, such as when you unexpectedly find yourself standing next to the colleague you want to influence by the lift, or bump into them in a corridor. Other opportunities will be in scheduled meetings which you know about in advance. On either occasion you may have just a few minutes to impress an influential colleague that what you have to say is worth hearing. Your challenge will be to select the words and arguments that will get the attention of your colleague early on, and sway their view toward considering seriously what you are saying.

It is vital that you are aware of the different values people use at work. You need to recognize the characteristics of the different sets of values, and be prepared to change your influencing arguments based on which values matter most to your colleagues. You need to step back from influencing situations that are scheduled as opposed to ad hoc, and plan how to approach each of them. For each situation that you prioritize in this way, you need to:

- Make an accurate assessment of the values of the colleagues with whom you will be speaking.
- Develop an influencing approach that addresses the issues that matter most to them.
- Convey your ideas in a manner that is tailored around their preferences for receiving information and processing that information.

The risks of not being able to do these things effectively are that you will miss the boat and:

- Fail to build influence with key colleagues at the time it matters most.
- Lose credibility with key opinion formers and senior colleagues.
- Find it difficult to secure further opportunities to build influence with them.

Chapter 4 focuses on how to position your arguments effectively so that they appeal to the different values of your senior colleagues. But for now, let's consider a different situation: that of mishandling the opportunity to build influence and suffering the consequences. The following case study highlights the reputational risks incurred by two junior equity partners in a law firm who fail to influence each other when working on a joint high-profile project.

CASE STUDY THREE: VALUING DIFFERENT THINGS

The regional partner-in-charge of a law firm is engaged in a pilot study to redesign the firm's internal mentoring program. The program assigns more junior equity partners to more experienced equity partners so that they can learn, develop, and be nurtured by their older, more knowledgeable colleagues. The regional partner-in-charge decides to offer two of his more ambitious junior equity partners the chance to work together on the project. It is a big opportunity for both of them. The project will involve them in consulting with and building credibility with senior figures in the firm, and he thinks they will both jump at the chance.

The regional partner-in-charge selects the two junior equity partners he wants to work together on the project. In making his selection he chooses two junior lawyers on the basis of their ambition and work ethic, two qualities that always impress him. He does not consider any other factors. The two colleagues work in different offices and only know each other by sight. The regional partner-in-charge briefs them together, gives them a clear timescale within which to complete the work, and warns them that it will be carried out under the noses of some of the most senior and influential people in the firm. He tells them that he has had his eye on both of them for a while, and that he is looking forward to following up with his senior colleagues and hearing good reports on how they conduct themselves. He tells them that he will let them decide how to approach the project, how to work together, and how to divide up the tasks that need to be accomplished. He also tells them that, should they need his input, he will gladly make time for them. Then he leaves them to it.

Let's take a look at the influencing styles of the two junior equity partners. The first junior equity partner has a clear preference for using the second influencing style. Her approach to influencing her colleagues involves presenting cogent, detail-oriented, factual arguments in a methodical and logical way. She is well respected by her clients for the accuracy of her legal advice and her thorough knowledge of the law. They regard her as being sober, serious, and credible. She is at her best when she has time to think through her arguments before giving a view, and tends, once she has formed a view, to be quite wedded to it. However, she is an able and astute lawyer, hard-working and dedicated. Provided that she is working with someone who is influenced by solely factual concerns, she is an effective co-worker. She enjoys her job because it enables her to work in an ordered and methodical way, to work alone for long periods of time, and to concentrate on getting the detail right. She derives considerable satisfaction from the self-sufficiency of her role and the rigor of her work. She regards her selection to work on the internal mentoring program as a pat on the back, but is also aware that she is in the spotlight. She doesn't want to mess up, and wants to make sure that she and her colleague take the time they need at the start of the project to ensure quality and avoid making errors.

The second junior equity partner uses a mixture of the first and third influencing styles. His approach to influencing a colleague focuses on generating momentum for the task in hand, emphasizing the exciting opportunities to be seized upon, highlighting the positive impact of his proposals for the business, and working to establish rapport with his co-worker. His clients respect him for his clear commitment to delivery. They see him as decisive, energetic, tough-minded, but also congenial and personable, a combination that wins him considerable loyalty from them. He derives satisfaction from being in a friendly, hard-working workplace, and has built a reputation as someone who is clearly focused on delivering the best and most effective service for his clients that he can. He is at his best when he has been given a clear remit and is left to get on with it his way. He enjoys his job for the challenge it provides him with, and because he works within a largely harmonious team. He regards his selection to work on the internal mentoring program as a sign of good faith. He thinks of the work as highly important for the firm, and feels sure that the outcomes of the project will be appreciated and valued by the regional partner-in-charge, a man he admires and wants to emulate. He values the opportunity that the project will afford him to meet and work with senior people in the firm, and he wants to take full advantage of these openings.

After an hour working together in a small office the two colleagues are making slow progress. They aren't working in tandem. Their relationship is characterized by bickering and squabbling, and occasional raised voices. The atmosphere in the room is marked by strain and intolerance, and by a heightened sense of unresolved tension. The problem is that the two colleagues cannot resolve their differences, and their attempts to influence one another are not bringing them together. Rather, they are forcing them farther apart.

Sure, the two colleagues have different ways of doing things and value divergent things. But instead of pooling their differing strengths to make an able team, their attempts to influence one another have made their differences more pronounced, not less so. Having expressed their divergent views on how best to go about approaching their joint project, the two of them then fail to find a way forward. Instead they waste a lot of time arguing about the merits of their different perspectives. They both claim that they want to work towards the same goal: to research and design an effective in-house mentoring program, and to build credibility with senior people as they do so. But, instead of getting on with it, they spend most of their time arguing about the differences between them.

Exasperated, the regional partner-in-charge decides to intervene after watching both of the colleagues walk out of their joint office at different times to take a breather. He arranges to speak with each colleague in turn, starting with the first junior equity partner. The first junior equity partner says that her more vigorous and sociable colleague disregards the practicalities of the project and doesn't want to plan. She says that he isn't pragmatic enough and is jeopardizing the quality of their joint work because of his impulsive nature. She states that he isn't prepared to work with her to devise a set of research questions for their conversations with potential mentors and mentees, and seems to want to simply leave the office to go and knock on the doors of people in the firm without having decided what to speak with them about. She complains that he keeps interrupting her for a chat, and regularly breaks her concentration while she is working. She says that when they first sat down to decide how best to work together, he diverged from the relevant issues of planning, prioritizing, and thinking about the most effective way of approaching the project, to debate how excited he was by the challenge before them and how useful the project would be in raising their profiles in the firm. She says he simply wastes time. She grumbles that she cannot seem to influence him to adopt a less impulsive and chatty approach, one characterized by more consistent, steady application and more thought. She comments that his attempts to influence her have taken on a more and more aggressive stance, one that has alienated and upset her.

When it is his turn to meet with his manager, the second junior equity partner says that his more rigorous colleague doesn't seem to want to get on with the work, but instead wants to draw up a detailed plan, a plan that is neither necessary nor useful in his opinion. He says that she holds up progress, doesn't make things happen, and is jeopardizing the progress of the project. He says that he wants to get out there and start talking to people, and is confident enough to do so without having to draw up a set of questions and issues to debate with them. He complains that his colleague won't let him adopt this approach, and wants to make sure that they have a predetermined list of subjects for the conversations they undertake to ensure a rigorous and unbiased process. He says that she is unfriendly, even rude, and that when he tries to speak with her about actually getting on with the work, she keeps reiterating the need to research and plan before doing anything, which is something he can't see the point of. He complains that he cannot seem to influence her to adopt a less cautious and more proactive approach, one that isn't so bogged down in paperwork, and that is more action-oriented and effective. He comments that the more he tries to influence her, the more remote and willful she becomes. He grumbles that he has given up trying to influence her because all she does is simply reiterate her point of view without being open to altering it.

As a result of his conversations with the two colleagues the regional partner-in-charge loses faith in them both. He hears their complaints about one another as two people bickering about personalities instead of taking advantage of the opportunity he has placed with them. He is distinctly unimpressed with them both. He decides that he does not want to waste any more time waiting for them to find a way to work productively together. He tells them that he is replacing them. His concern is to get the work completed on time and to standard, as he is aware that the other regions are waiting to see the results of the pilot project. He doesn't want to waste time, as he sees it, mediating between these two people. So he reassigns them to other less important work and replaces them with two new colleagues. Both the first junior equity partner and the second junior equity partner find this a very hard pill to swallow, and both of them are angry and upset by their manager's decision. Neither of them realizes that their approach to working together is the real problem, not their manager's conclusions about it.

The Opportunity to Influence

Let's examine the opportunities for the two junior equity partners to build influence in this scenario, starting with their relationships with their manager. Both of the junior lawyers have a significant opportunity to influence their manager by working together successfully on a high-profile project. They also have a significant opportunity to build their profiles with some of the most influential lawyers in the firm. Had they made a success of it, their regional partner-in-charge would have learned that he could trust them individually and as a duo, that he could rely on them to take on important work, handle it productively, and accomplish it effectively without needing much input from him. He and his senior colleagues would have been left with the impression that here were two hard-working, proactive, and capable lawyers, each of whom could well make a greater contribution to the firm in the future.

Both lawyers also have the opportunity to influence each other and learn from one another. The first junior equity partner has the opportunity to influence her colleague toward the view that some planning would be useful for their joint work, because it would enable them to ensure the quality of that work, measure progress, and keep track of how much they still have to do. Some planning would also enable them to provide the regional partner-in-charge with a meaningful update should he request one, and would give them a clear idea of how much work is before them and therefore how much time it will take to complete.

The second junior equity partner has the opportunity to influence his colleague toward the view that making headway and getting on with the work is vital if they are to be seen by their manager as delivery-focused and keen to take advantage of the opportunity they have been given. He has the opportunity to influence her toward realizing that starting the work earlier and without a completely thorough plan is in their interests, because it will enable them to demonstrate their keenness to carry out the work. He could also influence his colleague toward being a bit more sociable and slightly less standoffish, something that would help her feel more integrated and less separate from the rest of the team.

However, the two younger lawyers fail to influence one another, and then fail to convince the regional partner-in-charge that they have really tried to work well together. In fact, they find it so difficult to work together that they fall out, and handle their working relationship poorly enough that the regional partner-in-charge takes the project away from them. How does this happen?

Their relationships with one another suffer because neither of them is willing to see past their own preferences and values, and because both of them refuse to listen to the other. It is primarily a question of will, and both their wills are set against each other. Neither of them is willing to work with the agenda of the other at all, and both of them descend into a tug of war. They both turn their relationship into a battle about whose values and approach should prevail over the other's.

Sadly, neither of them learns anything from the outcome of the situation either. When the regional partner-in-charge removes the project from them, neither of them is able to take responsibility for their part in this decision. Both of them blame him for being unreasonable and hasty in his judgment of them, instead of looking at their own conduct to understand why he feels the need to act in this way.

Handling the Personalities

Both of the junior equity partners fail to take advantage of the opportunity they are given to work together well, and thereby lose the opportunity to win the admiration and good opinion of the opinion formers in the firm. Maybe their anxiety at being given such a high-profile project contributes to their intransigence with one another, but neither of them can avoid the conclusion that they mishandled a significant opportunity to build influence. Let's look in more detail at what they mishandled, starting with the misjudgments of the first junior equity partner.

The First Junior Equity Partner

The first younger lawyer believes that fact is the overriding principle in any influencing situation. However, she carries this belief too far and so fails to consider any of the other possible sets of influencing values. She discounts the role of opinion, as opposed to what she considers to be fact, and also discounts feelings, which she thinks irrelevant at work, when seeking to work with, influence, and engage with her colleague. She gives undue weight to her own view of what is and is not relevant to the project, and is dismissive, even peremptory, with the second junior equity partner, who wants to emphasize different factors, and who sees things from a different perspective. When the second junior equity partner wants her to respect and work with his values as well as her own, she refuses to listen to him. Instead of looking for a collaborative way forward she doesn't give him an inch, downplaying and even rejecting his differing values. She becomes more and more entrenched in her own view that the only way to handle the project is by thorough, rigorous upfront planning and a detailed, methodical approach. She imposes her need for method on him. Then she makes matters worse by isolating herself from her colleague when she refuses his overtures for an occasional chat. She considers these conversations to be a waste of time, and dismisses his requests as a distraction from the real work which she wants to get back to. Finally, she lets her need to remain, as she sees it, in control of the work cloud her judgment. She refuses to let her colleague apply himself to the actual work while she continues to plan how to carry it out.

What could she have done differently? The first junior equity partner would have helped her cause had she found it in herself to work with some of her colleague's values and some aspects of his agenda as well as pursuing her own firmly held preferences. She could have agreed to schedule coffee breaks so that his need to chat could be met in a way which didn't interrupt her work mid-flow. She could have agreed to spend a set amount of time personally planning how to handle the project, while simultaneously letting her colleague begin the work. She could have accepted his pleasure at carrying out work that benefited the firm and raised his profile, without seeing these as less valid reasons to come to work than her own.

The Second Junior Equity Partner

For his part the second junior equity partner could also have handled things quite differently. His first mistake is to not look past his own preferences and values, and recognize that his colleague's different strengths counterbalance his weaknesses. While being initially pleased at being asked to take on the challenge of redesigning the internal mentoring program, he doesn't think sufficiently about how to marry his strengths to the different and opposite strengths of his colleague. Like her, he allows the differences between them to become a point of dissent and conflict, instead of using them constructively. He interrupts her with unimportant comments which reflect his need to build rapport with her more than they contribute positively to their joint work. When she doesn't respond the way he wants, he begins to see her as unilateral and uncommunicative, and rather than alter his approach to working with her, he becomes increasingly persistent at trying to get her to chat. He fails to respect her need for privacy, and becomes more and more demanding of her. His attempts to influence her become more abrasive and impulsive and less effective, as he feels thwarted in his desire to make rapid progress and to work with a friendly co-worker. He begins to experience his colleague as someone who blocks progress, creates plans that detract from their work, and as someone who prevents him from directing the flow of the work in the way he needs to. As he feels more and more frustrated at what he considers to be her pedantic and finicky approach, he comes to regard his colleague as someone who is creating obstacles which prevent both of them from achieving the task they have been set to do. As a result he becomes more vigorous and somewhat angry in his dealings with her.

The second junior equity partner would have helped his own cause had he found a way to work with some of his colleague's values as well as his own. Instead he runs the risk of appearing to impose his own preferences on her without regard for the impact that this approach has on her or their joint work. He could have found it in himself to respect his colleague's need for space and time to think without interrupting her. He could have recognized the sense in doing some planning upfront, alongside his wish to simply start the work. He could have been less forceful in his attempts to influence her, and have relied on the quality of his arguments instead of his passion, or as she saw it aggression, to make his points. Finally, he could have listened more to her point of view and reflected back his understanding of it, rather than disregarding it and aggressively offering her his own divergent opinion instead.

The Outcome

The outcome for these two lawyers was poor indeed. They handled themselves in a way that did considerable damage to their credibility with the regional partner-in-charge, and injured their working relationships with one another. Their failure to work well together and to influence one another, even slightly, meant that they lost the opportunity to build credibility with senior influential lawyers in the firm, and left them both with tarnished reputations. Now they both have big tasks ahead of them if they are to convince their more senior colleagues that they are trustworthy members of the workforce and people they can rely on in future.

Conclusions

This case study highlights the pitfalls of failing to work constructively with the values and agenda of a colleague who uses a different influencing style to yours. It highlights how two people with opposing but potentially complementary strengths can let the differences between them become a point of conflict instead of a point of effective collaboration. In the case study two hard-working and talented lawyers become entrenched in their own viewpoints and fail to accommodate one another's different ways of doing things. They lack the basic will to try to influence one another in positive ways, and both come to believe that their approach is superior to the other person's, which they disregard.

The two lawyers lack the fundamental will to work well together. Had they decided early on in the project that they would do the hard work of sitting down and working out how to perform effectively by pooling their different strengths, had they been prepared to listen to one another, had they been prepared to see past their own preferences to some extent and accommodate one another, and had they each adopted effective influencing strategies, they may well have found a way to bring the project in on time and to standard. As it is, they fail to make the right choices, and pay a heavy price for their failure to work effectively together when the regional partner-in-charge takes the decision to remove the project from them both.

YOUR INFLUENCING BEHAVIOR

The case study illustrates that working well with another colleague is primarily a matter of will, and that the more divergent your values are, the more opportunity there is to see your colleague's strengths as mitigants against your own weaknesses. Having examined an example of two people who were not open to being influenced by one another let's now return to your influencing style.

Earlier on in the chapter you identified which sets of influencing values you normally use, and which further options you could call on if you need to. Let's now take that discussion one step further and explore the application of your influencing styles to your work in more detail. The following questions encourage you to select a specific colleague with whom you would like to build greater influence, and examine what adjustments to your natural style you might like to make to help you achieve this aim. You can jot down your answers to each of the following questions in the space below it:

■ Identify a colleague with whom you would like to develop greater influence but with whom you currently find it difficult to build influence. Which characteristics of your natural influencing styles, if any, does this colleague respond well to?

■ Which characteristics of your natural influencing style does this colleague not respond well to?

■ Given this analysis, what changes do you think you need to make to your natural influencing style if you are to develop greater influence with this colleague in the future?

Knowing who you want to build influence with is one thing. Being able to do it in a situation that matters to you is quite another. The following questions ask you to identify a specific situation in your workplace in which you would like to have greater influence with the colleague you have just considered. It is important that this same colleague is involved in the situation you want to examine, and has some say in whether or not you will be able to bring about the outcome you want. You might like to answer the following questions, jotting down your answers in the spaces below:

■ What is the situation in which you want to build greater influence?

■ What do you want to achieve in the situation?

■ From what you know of your colleague's approach to the issue, what do you think they are trying to achieve?

■ What do you want your colleague to think or say or do differently as a result of the influencing conversation you want to have with them?

■ So, what are the key factors that you need to emphasize in the influencing conversation you plan to have with them?

SUMMARY AND NEXT CHAPTER

This chapter focused on the values that underpin your influencing style. It encouraged you to make a distinction between the factors and issues that are likely to influence you, and the potentially different factors and issues that might influence your colleagues. The chapter suggested that the more you know about the personalities you are seeking to build influence with, the better placed you will be to adopt a strategy that proves persuasive with them. The chapter:

- Identified four distinctly different sets of influencing values, each of which has different characteristics and emphasizes different factors as important.
- Highlighted the need to select an influencing approach with your colleague's needs and preferences in mind, rather than your own.
- Explored the fact that arguments that are influential with you will not automatically prove persuasive with other people.
- Highlighted the value of designing the format of key influencing meetings to appeal to the values of the different people whose buy-in you need.
- Demonstrated that the starting point for building influence with a colleague is choosing to respect their preferences, values, and agenda, and working constructively with them.
- Examined the pitfalls of valuing your own values above a colleague's different values, thereby rejecting them.
- Included opportunities for you to apply the material to your own workplace relationships and a current issue.

Having highlighted these points we now need to get to grips with how you actually build influence and use influential behavior on a daily basis in your workplace. The next chapter discusses the issues involved when you try to influence a colleague to adopt your views on a particular issue, and find that, no matter how obvious what you are saying is to you, they simply don't get it.

CHAPTER 4

Positioning Your Argument

You have formed a view on an issue that is important to you, but without the backing of key colleagues for your ideas, plans, or proposals, you cannot move ahead. You decide to speak with them so that you can influence them toward your point of view. You know what you want to say and how you want to say it. Your arguments make complete sense to you. Adopting your proposals will result in clear benefits to your organization, its customers, your work, and/or the work being done by your colleague or colleagues whose buy-in you need. But when it comes to it, no one else gets what you are saying. You are frustrated to realize that your attempts to influence your colleagues toward your way of thinking are not working. Your words are crystal clear and your arguments compelling as far as you are concerned. What you have said and how you have said it make total sense to you, but you are hitting a brick wall as far as your colleagues are concerned. Your views are dismissed, sometimes immediately, and at other times they are considered in insufficient detail to leave you satisfied that you have been heard. You are stymied and you don't know why.

This chapter will focus on the frustrating situation of finding out that what is blatant and significant to you is apparently a side-issue or opaque to others. It will explore how subtle but powerful adjustments in the way in which you position your argument can help you win the day. It will examine how to organize your argument so that it appeals to the colleagues whom you wish to influence, even those who have a reputation for being hard to influence. It will highlight how a clear understanding of what will prove pivotal in the minds of your colleagues, rather than what compels you, can help you avoid the exasperating situation where you actually lose credibility with more influential people through a failed attempt to influence them even though right is on your side.

This chapter will therefore focus on how to construct your arguments, which aspects of them to emphasize, and how to go about positioning your views with the colleagues you want to influence. It will help you to step back from your day-to-day work and:

■ Reassess the way in which you approach influencing conversations.

■ Highlight a range of reasons why an argument that you consider to be clear-cut might fail to influence a particular colleague.

■ Develop your awareness of which factors tend to prove more influential with which colleagues.

■ Give you the best chance of building influence with key colleagues in the situations that matter most to you.

WHY CAN'T THEY SEE IT?

Let's set the scene by exploring the issues involved when one colleague decides to influence their manager and finds that their proposition, while making perfect sense in their own mind, doesn't influence their senior colleague at all. Consider the following examples:

■ A relatively new secondary school teacher wants to take the children in her inner-city class on a day out along the canal. This particular school doesn't organize trips away from the school premises as part of its curriculum, and the teacher is excited at the thought of introducing a new and stimulating item to the school syllabus. She researches the costs of hiring a coach to take the children to the canal and of hiring a canal boat for the day. She asks several parents for their informal reaction to the proposed trip, and encouraged by their positive comments, decides to approach the head with her suggestion. She arranges to meet the school principal in her office. During their meeting the secondary school teacher emphasizes the benefits to the children as she sees it: the fun they'd have on the canal, the opportunity to get to know one another outside the school premises, the enjoyment to be derived from being in a rural location on a sunny day, a break from the urban environment they live in. The head barely hears her, and dismisses her suggestion with a curt 'That isn't going to happen.' Initially the secondary school teacher is taken aback. She assumes that the head must have misunderstood her, so she starts to go through it all again. The head interrupts her, and tells her that the suggestion is 'idle and foolish.' She asks her to leave her office 'so she can get back to work.'

■ The head of internal audit in a building society wants to take his management team of four people on a one-day team-building event. It is a particularly trying time for the building society, and the internal audit team has a high workload to manage. The head of internal audit thinks his management team need planned time away together. He prepares a business-focused agenda, speaks to a facilitator about hosting the event, and gathers costs together for holding the workshop at a local country house hotel. Then he approaches his boss for the budget he needs to pay for the event. He outlines his aims and objectives for the day, emphasizing that his team need to step back from their work, spend time together reassessing their goals and objectives, deepen their business relationships, and refocus their joint efforts around the priorities before them. He is amazed to hear his boss say, 'What do you want to do that for?'

■ A customer services manager in a large soft drinks manufacturer wants to change the way in which her team handle new orders and after-sales queries. At present they arrive via email, via the company's website, and over the phone. She wants to rearrange her team so that, instead of designated people picking up telephone calls, email messages, or messages routed via the website, any member of the team can respond to any incoming method of enquiry. The customer services manager believes that this way of working will prevent interruptions to service delivery during tea, coffee, and lunch breaks, and thinks that it will make the work of each team member more varied, more stimulating, and more interesting. She also believes it will create a climate in the team whereby everyone pulls together, rather than the present situation where the three teams compete with one another. She approaches the HR director to whom she reports, and tells him that she has an idea to improve teamwork and collaboration in the team. She begins to outline her idea to him, but is surprised to be interrupted by him. He tells her that he is busy and doesn't have time for team reorganizations. He asks her to leave so he can make an urgent phone call.

In each of these examples a perfectly good idea is rejected by a more senior and influential colleague, someone whose say-so is imperative if the main characters' plans are to become reality. In two of the scenarios the central character doesn't even manage to outline their plans in full before being silenced. Why has each character been unable to find the words to convey the sense and business benefits of their plans to their more senior colleague? Put simply, it's because they:

- Didn't position their arguments effectively enough.
- Didn't manage the perceptions that they created in the minds of their senior managers carefully enough.
- Emphasized the wrong arguments as they presented their proposals.
- Started their meetings in the wrong place.

GAINING BUY-IN TO KEY PROPOSALS

Let's revisit each example.

The First Example

In the first example the secondary school teacher makes a fundamental mistake in emphasizing the social and health benefits to the children of spending time together on the canal. She uses the relationship and process-oriented third influencing style, and as a supportive mentor to her students, wants to use the day out to promote friendship, fun, and relaxed social activity. She believes that the more relaxed, happy, and healthy a child is, the more likely it is that they will want to learn. The head, however, is not persuaded by this line of argument, and is peremptory in her dismissal of the new teacher's suggestion. Why?

The head has a strong preference for the factual, data-centered, and goal-oriented second influencing style. Her overriding concerns are to ensure high-quality education for the students, and to manage and eliminate areas of risk to the children and the school. She regards herself as an educator, and sees education as being primarily about the syllabus and core curriculum against which the school's performance will be measured. She hears her teacher's analysis of the benefits of the day out only in terms of a fun day for the teachers and students who go on the trip, something she thinks of as largely unimportant. She also hears her more junior colleague's presentation of the day out only in terms of her own fears. Her fears include the unmanaged risks inherent in taking the children away from the school for a day out on a canal. She is afraid of the health and safety issues and the insurance implications. She is particularly aware that recent news items have focused on the backlash that teachers have faced after children in their care were injured on a school expedition. She is worried that some of the more unscrupulous parents might use any mishaps, real or imagined, to sue her or the school, or make trouble for her with the school governors. When she is listening to the teacher outlining her plans, these fears rush through her head in a split second. Also, the school doesn't have any day trips on its current curriculum, and the head doesn't feel safe introducing such a measure out of the blue. It's too new, too novel, and not tied into anything the school currently does. She is busy and stressed, and is a somewhat cynical character. Instead of explaining her reasoning to the new teacher, she decides to put down her socially conscious and, as she sees it, touchy feely member of staff, and focus instead on her priority for the day, which is keeping the government inspectors happy. She says somewhat cuttingly that she has to 'get back to work.'

However, it is not true to say that just because these two members of staff have different ways of looking at the world, they cannot work well together. Had the secondary school teacher positioned her argument differently she *would* have stood a good chance of influencing the head to at least consider her proposal. To achieve this aim she needs to start the meeting in a different place.

She needs to position her arguments to appeal to the head's preference for goal-oriented, well-planned, and well-managed education projects; and she needs to address the head's fears fully at the beginning of her influencing conversation. The teacher needs to make it clear that her plans carry some risk, but that in her view the risks are manageable, and can be born primarily by the school's insurance policies. The teacher needs to wait until she is sure that the school head has taken this point on board before proceeding to outline the remainder of her plans in factual terms.

She needs to emphasize the teaching and educational benefits of the trip rather than its social benefits, perhaps highlighting how the trip could be used in conjunction with geography, social history, and biology options. Also, she would do well to produce some data to show that other schools in the area arrange off-campus trips, while explaining what they do, how they do it, how often, and for which age groups. She would have helped her cause had she used the meeting to gauge the head's reaction to her plans bit by bit as she unfolded them, rather than excitedly speak about them all at once, assuming that she would be heard and understood. That way she might have picked up on her head's concerns, and addressed them, rather than run the risk of being characterized as naïve and idealistic. She could also have presented the head with a written summary of her plans so that she could read them after the meeting.

These are subtle differences to make, but to someone like the head who is only influenced by a small number of pivotal factors, such as educational benefits, managed risks, and child safety, they are key alterations to make.

The Second Example

The head of internal audit makes a fundamental mistake in approaching his boss for the budget for the one-day off-site meeting he wants to hold. He assumes that his boss will be persuaded by the same factors that prove persuasive with him. The head of internal audit uses a combination of the first and third styles. He wants to make rapid progress against his goals, but he also wants to take people with him, building harmonious relationships with his team members wherever possible. He values his workplace relationships and understands the role of teamwork in effective delivery. He wants to make sure that his team members have the opportunity to talk through their concerns with the heavy workload that they are being asked to shoulder. However, his boss uses only the first style, and has one pre-eminent concern, which takes precedence in his mind over all other matters. His concerns are to deliver on time and to standard, and he expects his team members to generate and maintain momentum on the projects they manage. Anything that he perceives as being likely to prevent rapid progress against goals, waste time, or slow down momentum will annoy him. He will not see the point of it, and will say so bluntly and directly. Sadly for him, the head of internal audit presents his case primarily in terms of building relationships, and his boss is not persuaded by those arguments at all.

However, had he positioned his argument differently, the head of internal audit could have succeeded in gaining a budget for his off-site meeting. To do so, he needs to start his meeting with his manager in a different place by outlining his understanding of his boss's priorities. He could say that he is aware of the huge pressure to deliver that the group are under, before telling his boss that he wants to talk to him about an idea he has to streamline delivery over the next few months. Having got his boss's attention, he could then outline his business-focused agenda for the team-building event, omitting the points about building relationships, and instead emphasizing that the time will be used to plan and prioritize for the busy upcoming quarter. He could stress that the off-site event he is planning will enable him and his team to be more effective at directing both their own work and the work of their more junior colleagues, as well as ensuring that the team makes rapid progress against its goals. This approach is more likely to appeal to a man who is quick to form a view, unlikely to alter it once it has been made, and who is primarily influenced by plans and proposals that improve his department's ability to produce high-quality work.

The Third Example

The customer services manager approaches the HR director with a plan to reorganize her team, improving its capacity to respond to incoming enquiries, and preventing the petty competition which affects all three sections of the team at the moment. She is surprised and dismayed to find that her ideas receive a curt and final 'no'. She has misjudged the character of the HR director, and used the wrong approach it discuss her plans with him.

The customer services manager uses a combination of the second and third influencing styles. She is goal-oriented and values achieving her targets in a high-quality, meticulous way. But she also wants to invest in her relationships with her team members and provide them with stimulating work if at all possible. Her plans therefore appeal very much to her mindset. However, the HR director is influenced by very different concerns from hers, concerns which she doesn't address at all during her presentation of her ideas to him. While he does see the sense of what she is saying, the HR director is not influenced by her proposals.

The HR director uses a mixture of the first and fourth styles. He is highly motivated to make rapid progress against his targets, but is also influenced by opportunities to enhance his prestige and profile around the company. In fact he is highly concerned for his own image with his peers and managers. When managing his own profile with his bosses he wants to appear capable, politically astute, and a sure pair of hands. Crucially, he knows something that the customer services manager does not know. He knows that the board is planning a major reorganization which will affect every team in the company. As soon as the customer services manager mentions the word 'reorganization' and begins to outline her plans, he stops her. His concern is that any reorganization he sponsors will appear ill-considered and potentially be seen as an attempt to undermine his bosses. He forms the instant view that if he supports the customer services manager's proposals he will inevitably portray himself to his bosses as lacking politically, and lose their respect. He cannot afford to do so, but equally he cannot reveal to the customer services manager why he rejects her proposals. So he says he has an urgent call to make instead.

If we accept that she is unaware of the behind-the-scenes plans for a major reorganization, what could the customer services manager have done to gain the support of her manager for her own reorganization? She also needs to start the conversation in a different place. She needs to start it with him and not with her own plans. She would do well to ask him what she could be doing to make the work of her team more valuable to him. This opening would prepare him for the fact that she might have something interesting to offer. His reply would give her valuable information to work with, as she thinks on her feet and positions her subsequent proposals with him. He might say that he would like her team to deliver quicker, or with fewer errors, or achieve more work in less time. She is then free to position her plans as likely to achieve these aims. For instance, she could say that she would like to speak with him about a way of rearranging the team so that less time is wasted in competition. Or she could say that she has an idea to ensure that more work is achieved on any given day, or that she has a proposal for making sure that more customers are satisfied first time with the response they get to their enquiry. Given the major reorganization that is planned by his bosses, the HR director may still feel disinclined or unable to give her plans the go-ahead straight away. But he would be highly motivated to represent them upwards to his bosses, securing for himself the kudos of adding value to their evolving reorganization plans. The customer services manager may well find that some months down the road her team reorganization is given the go-ahead.

All three of the examples we have been considering involve an attempt by the main character to influence their boss in a one-to-one meeting. In each case the influencing style that the main character uses does not prove influential with their more senior colleague, and the way in which they position their argument falls flat. All the strengths of their argument, as they see it, are regarded as weaknesses by their senior colleague, and they lose credibility in a situation in which they could reasonably have expected to gain it. All three of these examples highlight how important it is to think carefully about the person you want to influence in advance of going to speak to them, so that you:

- Recognize what your arguments *will mean to them* given their values and work style, as opposed to what they mean to you, given your values and work style.
- Start the meeting with them, their goals, and their concerns.
- Position your proposals to appeal to their priorities.

Using this approach will make it much more likely that you:

- Avoid the pitfall of appearing out of touch with your boss's agenda.
- Avoid their subsequent value judgments about you, should your boss perceive your plans to be unimportant or irrelevant.
- Give yourself the best chance of influencing them toward the merits of your case.

You may experience many of the influencing situations you find yourself in as being less clear-cut than the examples quoted above. But, even if the colleague you want to influence does share some values with you, or looks at some issues in a similar way to you, you would still do well to implement the approach I am advocating here if you are to maximize your chances of securing influence with them.

YOUR INFLUENCING BEHAVIOR

You may now like to identify a situation in which you failed to build influence at work. The colleague involved could be senior to you or a peer of yours. Bring a specific situation to mind and then answer the following questions about it. You can jot down your answers to each of the questions in the space below it:

- Thinking about that specific situation, who did you want to influence and in what way?

- How did you position your argument with them? What key points did you emphasize?

■ Referring to the sets of values introduced in the previous chapter, which values or combination of values do you think your colleague uses?

■ Looking back on it now, why do you think your arguments did not prove influential with this colleague?

■ What changes would you make to the way you positioned your influencing argument should you have the opportunity to hold the conversation again?

Having examined an example of where you failed to influence one of your key colleagues toward your way of thinking, let's now turn our attention to a different situation. This situation is one in which you need to secure the buy-in of a number of different people, each of whom is vital to the success of your plans. You know each of these people quite well, partly because they are your peer group, but also because you and your teams work together quite closely. You consider that you have an existing, functioning relationship with your peers, and that the influence this quality of relationship affords you should be sufficient to enable you to get done the things you need to achieve. Let's examine the issues by taking a look at a longer example, which is set in the technology group of an investment bank.

CASE STUDY FOUR: THE GO-BETWEEN

A technology manager in an investment bank decides that he wants to change the way in which his team and his three peers' teams respond to requests for technical support from the front office which they jointly support. Currently, front office traders log their requests for technology support with the helpdesk. The helpdesk is manned on a rotating basis by members of all four teams. Calls are picked up in sequential order by the next available technologist, who then responds to the query straight away. However, recently several members of the highly pressurized front office have complained about the slow speed of response to some of their requests for assistance. They are unhappy about what they see as unacceptable delays following urgent requests for technology support, and about their perception that certain technologists seem unable or unwilling to change direction rapidly enough to reprioritize more urgent items over less urgent items. As a result some front office contacts have resorted to using more demanding and more unreasonable behavior when talking with their technology colleagues. The technology manager observes all these trends, and as a result of the increasing pressure being applied to the technologists in the four teams, he decides to act.

The technology manager uses a combination of the first two styles. He is highly goal-oriented, concerned to generate momentum while keeping things moving, and keen to get the detail right too. He is concerned for the quality of the work he does and the efficiency with which he does it. He speaks with a number of people from each of the teams to identify what they think of their front office customers. His informal research reveals that his own team members think their business colleagues to be, variously, unrealistic about practical considerations and risks, likely to jump to conclusions, and likely to change their goals, plans and proposals on a regular basis. His conversations with his peers' teams reveal similar views. They say that front office staff members are likely to be impulsive, insufficiently cautious, and highly imprudent. They regard them as blunt to the point of rude, and at times unnecessarily castigating. The manager forms the view that to the cautious, methodical, and exact mind of a technologist, these are stressful inter-personal characteristics to have to deal with on a day-to-day basis.

However, the technology manager is also keen to understand the perspective of the front office. He arranges a series of short interviews with a range of front office customers so that he can ask them for their perceptions about the technology team. He hears a catalogue of complaints. They say that the technology team members are slow to respond to urgent front office demands. They complain that the technologists are driven by processes and procedures, become bogged down with details, and are likely to put obstacles in the way of progress. They protest at the tendency of the technologists to keep asking for more information instead of acting, and at what they see as a consistent failure by the technologists to generate momentum on the projects and fixes they are charged with handling. Finally, they say that their technology colleagues don't live in the real world, are remote from the urgent realities of front office life, and represent a costly overhead for the business.

The technology manager is under no illusions about the size of the task before him if he is to bring these two sets of people together so that they can work more effectively for the good of their employer. He is aware that if the front office perception of his team doesn't improve soon he and his peers will be asked to account for these perceptions and complaints, probably by a senior trading manager. Equally, he thinks that the four technology teams might be hard pressed to adopt the more vigorous and punchy style that seems to be required if they are to gain the respect of their front office contacts. He decides that he, in the first instance, must influence his three peers toward a new way of working with the front office and puts his thinking cap on.

He arranges a meeting with his three peers. Believing that he has sufficient influence with this group of people that he will be able to influence them toward addressing the front office feedback, the technology manager prepares for the meeting. He thinks that all of his peers favor the second influencing style. They are cautious, exact, and quality-conscious people who are highly goal-oriented and logical in their approach to their work. The technology manager wants to use the meeting to influence his colleagues that they need to act. He wants them to take a series of measures which will result in the front office becoming more positive about the quality of service it receives from the four technology teams. He doesn't want to get into how they will accomplish this goal during the meeting, merely to get to a point of agreement among the four of them that they will act together to bring about an incremental improvement in the quality of response they collectively offer to the front office.

The technology manager thinks about how best to position his arguments with his three peers, and plans his strategy. He forms the view that the issues are both clear-cut and unassailable. He starts the meeting by outlining the key issues as he sees them. He tells his peers that he wants to see the technology team achieve tighter delivery deadlines in a more cost-effective manner. He says he would like them to respond more rapidly to urgent escalations and deprioritize less important escalations, while still completing those fixes in a timely manner. He then says that he wants to see the technology team adopt a more assertive, proactive, and enthusiastic demeanor when handling their front office contacts, and that he wants them to appear both action-oriented and committed to excellence.

He pauses for a moment and then finishes by saying that over the next few months he would like to get to a place where the front office talks about the excellent value for money it receives from the technology teams. He says that he would like to use the current meeting to explore ways in which to achieve these interconnected and top-priority aims. He is surprised at the length of silence which follows his opening remarks, and amazed when his three colleagues continue to look blankly at him, apparently having nothing to say. He makes eye contact with each of them, but is dismayed to realize that they have no interest in the content of the meeting so far. It appears to have left them cold even though, as he sees it, it fairly and squarely affects them. Finally, after a lengthy pause, one of them asks him what he expects of them, in a tone that conveys his total lack of interest in, or appreciation of, the issues the technology manager has just spoken about.

It becomes clear to the technology manager that none of his three colleagues sees the point of the meeting, and none of them has been influenced by his analysis of the issues before them. He leaves the meeting worried that he might have lost some of the influence he had with this group of peers, or worse, might have completely misjudged his relationships with them and never have had any influence with them in the first place.

The Opportunity to Influence

In this case study the technologist has a significant opportunity to influence his three peers, their teams, and then ultimately the highly influential front office, the senior trading bosses, and his own bosses. To achieve these outcomes he has to succeed in altering sufficient front office colleagues' perceptions about the quality of service they receive from the technology team. If he succeeds in influencing his customer base, or enough of them, that the technology team are effective and able internal suppliers, he stands to build a reputation as someone who:

- Can be trusted by the highly influential front office.
- Can take poorly performing technology teams and turn them around.
- Can successfully liaise between the energetic, hard-to-impress front office and the more reticent technology teams.
- Implements projects that improve the front office and the bank's capacity to make money.
- Is an able facilitator and possesses an effective suite of influencing and people-handling skills.
- Is an active, solutions-focused member of the workforce.

However, should he fail to inspire his peers to join with him in improving their teams' performance, his credibility will take a major hit. He has already spoken to a range of front office customers about their perceptions of the technology team. Each of these customers will now be expecting action as a result of their meeting with him, and if he fails to deliver, they will likely be more annoyed with him and his team than had he not spoken with them in the first place. Equally, his credibility with his peer group will also suffer. Rather than being seen as someone who has used his existing influence with them wisely to make needed changes to their joint service, he will be regarded as someone who made a wrong move and lost some of the influence he had previously gained.

Handling the Personalities

In order to succeed with his plans to influence his peers, the technology manager has to present his analysis in a way that appeals to three people who see things differently from him. He needs to demonstrate to each of his technology team peers that his proposals will benefit their teams, their customers, and themselves, and that they will be achievable. Sadly for him, his management of the initial meeting doesn't achieve any of these aims, and he doesn't generate any interest at all in his plans. All this is despite the fact that what he said was wholly true, clearly thought out, and well presented. What went wrong?

The technology manager presented his opening remarks as a series of statements of fact. He told his three peers that:

- The front office is not comfortable with the level of service it is receiving.
- Several front office colleagues have concerns about the style of service delivery, the speed of response, and the prioritization of fixes.
- These front office colleagues question the inter-personal skills and the resolve of the technologists they deal with, as well as the cost-effectiveness of maintaining such a large technology presence in-house.
- He would like to engineer sufficient service improvements that these front office contacts start to speak regularly about the excellent value for money they receive from the technology teams.
- He would like his peers to join him in bringing about this shift in perception by implementing a series of well-planned and carefully targeted service enhancements.

It never occurred to the technology manager that these, as he sees it, statements of fact were perceptions that his peers might not concur with. Nor did it occur to him that, even if they think there is some truth in what he is saying, his colleagues might not be motivated to acknowledge the truth of these perceptions openly or address the issues publicly. As they are polite and courteous people, they didn't interrupt him or question him while he was speaking. Instead they waited for him to complete what he was saying, and then looked blankly at him. Finally, one of them asked him what the relevance was of what he had been saying to them.

In order to succeed the technology manager needs to adopt a completely different approach to the meeting. Firstly, he needs to speak to each of his three peers *before* the meeting, either in a phone call or in a one-to-one meeting. These courtesy calls will create the opportunity for him to feed back the front office's perceptions of service delivery to each peer privately, and will consequently avoid the possibility of embarrassing any of his colleagues in front of their peers. Crucially, separate one-to-one meetings will provide the technology manager with the chance to gauge each person's reaction to the feedback, as well as enable him to listen to their opinion about the front office's reported perceptions. Had he taken this route he would have heard:

- His first peer expressing annoyance and irritation at another set of unfounded criticisms by front office staff.
- The second peer saying that his team are working flat out and don't have the capacity to do things differently.
- His third peer stating that he would like to address the issues that have been raised but can't see his other colleagues being as enthusiastic as he is.

Having elicited their initial reactions to the feedback the technology manager then needs to introduce some structure into the one-to-one conversation. The structure will encourage his peer to engage with the feedback and think through some of its implications in a more deep and measured way. It will encourage him to get past his initial first reactions and consider the feedback more fully.

The technology manager could ask each peer what surprises him about the feedback, and what he specifically agrees and disagrees with. He might also ask each peer what he considers to be the priorities for action, and which issues he thinks will matter most to the front office. He might go on to suggest that it would be in their interests to call a four-way meeting at which to make progress on the issues, and that he is prepared to manage and lead that meeting, but that he really needs his colleague's input at it. Then he can suggest a suitable time and date.

It is highly unlikely that his colleague will refuse to attend, and armed with all three peers' reactions to the feedback, the technology manager will be much better placed to use the four-way meeting creatively and constructively. Firstly, each peer will have had time to reflect on the feedback before attending the group meeting, and won't be surprised by the extent of the criticisms. Secondly, none of them will be able to avoid responsibility for responding to the feedback by sitting silently and waiting for their colleagues to speak. This tactic proved effective at blocking progress during the first meeting, and completely threw the technology manager. Using this new approach this outcome could not happen, as all three peers will be familiar with the feedback and will have elected to attend a meeting to address it. Thirdly, the technology manager could use the group meeting to find solutions to the issues affecting service delivery, instead of talking about the criticisms that the front office has made about the technology team.

The technology manager still has much work to do at the group meeting if he is to secure the kind of response he wants from his colleagues. He will need to use a carefully crafted, measured approach throughout the meeting. He is dealing with a group of people who are risk averse, who hide in difficult meetings, and who don't respond well to criticism. He needs to influence three peers who are comfortable with stability and who like routine, to change the style, structure, and emphasis of their teams' way of handling front office escalations. This will not be an easy thing to accomplish, but he does stand some chance of achieving this goal if he structures his meetings around the needs and preferences of his colleagues rather than around his own different and punchier style. How does he need to handle this meeting?

He needs to start the meeting by thanking his colleagues for attending and telling them that he sees the meeting as an opportunity for him to touch base with them as a group following his recent one-to-one conversations with them. He could then tell them that, having listened to their feedback, he has identified three specific priorities for action. He could explain that each of the priorities involves their teams in doing things differently and better, and that the changes he proposes will be worth it because they will obviate some of the major criticisms leveled at them recently by the front office. He could say that he would like to run through each of the changes he proposes and get their views on them.

This approach will gain their interest because he is taking responsibility for moving the project forward and doesn't expect them to. He is asking for their views on specific issues rather than asking for public reaction to negative feedback; he sounds confident that they can make progress in the one meeting rather than creating the impression that he might need a lot of their time. Also, he is promising his peers tangible benefits from working with him, benefits such as reduced flak from the front office, improved praise from the front office, reduced management time spent responding to and managing adverse client perceptions, and the prestige to be garnered from having improving service delivery to the influential front office.

The technology manager could then present the first of his suggestions for improving service delivery, and get his peers' feedback on the practical feasibility of the idea. After they have discussed the idea he could give them some time to think through the implications of the proposed change for their teams. He might call a tea and coffee break to give them some thinking time. He needs to let them absorb the information, make links between it and their own previously articulated views, and consider its implications for their team, before he asks them to move on. Only after having taken them through this thinking process, one designed to be comfortable for them and therefore to enable them to work well with him, should he move on to the second of his suggestions.

The Outcome

In this scenario the technology manager's approach to the first meeting, while making complete sense to him, doesn't sit comfortably with his peers, whom he loses right at the start of the meeting. However, he is highly motivated to try again, as he doesn't wish to let the front office down by failing to deliver on his promise to improve the quality of service. His second attempt is more influential, and he builds sufficient commitment from his peers that they implement the three ideas he presents to them within two weeks of the group meeting. Front office feedback is positive, although they are not yet satisfied that the standard of service is as consistently high as they require. The technology manager continues to act as go-between with the front office and the technology teams, and over time, succeeds in gaining support for further service improvement measures. However, it is a big job, and he needs to keep on top of his peers' tendency to downplay or ignore front office feedback so that they can carry on with the day's work uninterrupted. He has his work cut out but is determined to succeed.

Conclusions

This case study demonstrates how to secure buy-in from a group of reticent but hard-working peers while doing so in a way that retains and extends the level of influence that a technology manager has with them. It illustrates that, if he is to prevail in the second and subsequent group meetings, the technology manager needs to use an approach that starts with the perceptions of his peers, not with the perceptions of the front office, or his own conclusions about the front office feedback he has gathered. In planning for these meetings with his peers, the technology manager needs to adopt a step-by-step approach. He needs to take his peers through a process of analyzing data, absorbing that data, and coming to a conclusion about it, before asking them to consider what action to take. Any other approach will run the risk of appearing irrelevant to them, unappealing to them, or unreasonably stretching of them, and won't get their buy-in. But should he adopt a steady, planned approach he stands a good chance of being able to influence a group of people who are naturally interested in doing high-quality work, and who will be motivated to adopt changes provided the meeting is handled in a way that is helpful to them.

YOUR INFLUENCING BEHAVIOR

We have just explored an example which features an employee initially struggling to influence his peers before changing his approach and succeeding. You may now like to identify a situation in which you struggled to build influence with your peers. Bring a specific situation to mind, then answer the following questions about it. You can jot down your answers to each of the questions in the space below it:

- Thinking about that specific situation, which peers did you want to influence and in what way?

- How did you position your arguments with them? What key points did you emphasize?

■ Looking back on it now, why do you think positioning your arguments in this way did not prove influential?

■ What changes would you make to the way you position your arguments should you have the opportunity to hold the conversation again?

SUMMARY AND NEXT CHAPTER

This chapter has focused on how to position your argument for maximum effect with your manager or your peers. It:

■ Highlighted how arguments that make sense to you can prove ineffective at influencing your colleagues.
■ Examined how making subtle but important changes to the way in which you position your arguments can make all the difference to your gaining the buy-in you want.
■ Explored how building influence is about what your plans and proposals mean to the people you want to influence, rather than what they mean to you, where the two sets of perceptions are different.
■ Suggested that it is important to pre-position feedback or important information with colleagues rather than run the risk of losing them in a group meeting.
■ Identified how to plan influencing conversations so that the process of the meeting gives the colleagues you want to influence the best

chance of understanding, processing, and working constructively with the points you want to make.

■ Included an opportunity for you to apply the material to your working life.

The next chapter explores how to build and retain influence in situations where you are under pressure to act in ways that don't sit comfortably with your values, or that conflict with your sense of the difference between right and wrong.

CHAPTER 5

Moral Conflicts: Your Resolve Under Pressure

There are many situations at work where what you need to do or what you mustn't do is both clear-cut and obvious. Most of the time you get paid to do the right thing, and your role involves you in determining what the right course of action is in any situation before implementing it. However, sometimes what your managers, other colleagues, and from time to time clients, expect of you isn't in line with either your own values, or on occasion the law. In some of these cases your boss, your co-workers, or your customers might want you to behave in ways that conflict with your values, your natural, innate sense of the difference between right and wrong, or your sense of what is the best course of action for your team or organization. Responding to these situations means building influence with difficult and often more senior colleagues in situations where you need to protect your core values, and where you are being pressurized into taking actions with which you fundamentally disagree. These are the issues that this chapter will address.

The chapter will focus on the challenging situation of realizing that what is expected of you by either your senior colleagues or your internal clients is not acceptable to you. It will explore the options before you should you find yourself in this situation, and it will outline the areas in which you do have room for maneuver. It will examine how important it is to try and build influence in these situations, rather than to comply with what you know to be wrong. It will highlight how being prepared to stand your ground in certain pivotal situations is essential if you are to retain any influence at all with the senior managers or internal clients involved, and sometimes if you are to protect your well-being as well.

The chapter will examine the pitfalls and consequences for you of failing to stand up for what you think is right, and will explore how you could render yourself powerless at work should you continue to defer unwisely over a period of time. The chapter will focus on the challenge of having to find effective influencing arguments at the precise time you are asked to take actions that you think are unwise or simply wrong, both in situations where there isn't anyone else to whom you can escalate the issues, and where escalating could be a course of action you pursue.

The chapter will help you to step back from your day-to-day work and:

- Recognize the importance of marshalling your resolve and choosing to engage with challenging issues in order to build influence in the most demanding of situations.
- Clarify a range of factors that you could use to help you determine where to draw the line with a boss or internal client.
- Give yourself the best chance of acting in effective and influential ways should you find yourself asked to implement decisions you do not believe in.

DOING THE 'RIGHT THING'

Most of the time your job will involve you in work that is clear-cut and simple morally, even if it can become complicated inter-personally from time to time. The parameters within which you need to work to accomplish the tasks before you will mainly be unambiguous, and the limits within which you need to keep will be well established. Indeed these boundaries will often provide clarity, and differentiate what is acceptable from what is not. Consider the following examples:

- A motor mechanic is employed to test a fleet of vehicles on a yearly basis for his employer to determine which cars are roadworthy and which are not. He decides to fail a particular vehicle he has been testing. The car's brake system is faulty and the mechanic considers that it represents a hazard to the colleague driving it and to other road users. He fails the vehicle and calls the manager of the department concerned. He tells him that he will only give it a roadworthiness certificate after its brakes have been overhauled and it has passed a subsequent retest. The department manager leaves his office immediately and goes to see the motor mechanic. He walks toward him, smiles and asks him to turn a blind eye. The mechanic refuses with a shake of the head. The manager says that has to get a series of deliveries out that day and needs the vehicle straight away. The mechanic refuses him a second time. He seeks to influence the manager toward the view that the brakes could fail at any time and that in that eventuality the driver, who is one of his team members, and other road users will be put at risk. He tells the manager that he cannot issue a road-worthiness certificate and will not turn a blind eye. On hearing this same answer again the manager gets angry. He takes another step toward the mechanic and says in a more menacing tone that he wants the vehicle to pass its test even with its faulty brakes. The mechanic takes a step back and again refuses with a shake of the head. The manager takes another step forward and says he will report the matter to the mechanic's boss. The mechanic tells him that that will be fine and that his boss will say the same thing. Then he retains the keys for the vehicle and signals to his boss, who is working in his glass-fronted office, to join them.

■ An internal auditor is conducting an audit of a trading area in a bank. He is concerned by a number of his findings, and forms the view that the trading environment is not as secure as he would like it to be. He is particularly worried by two settlement issues, and considers that either of them poses a significant risk to the bank should anyone want to take advantage of the loopholes, or should monies be mislaid. He approaches the trading desk head to speak about his findings, and is dismayed to receive a cutting and cold response from the desk head, who says she is too busy to deal with trivialities. The auditor says that he cannot let the matter rest and will need to pursue it. When asked why, he simply tells the trading desk head that it is his job to ensure the safety of the trading environment, and that he is not satisfied. She greets this comment with a withering look, and returns to her paperwork, effectively dismissing the auditor. He refuses to be sidelined, and despite the fact that she is bending to her work in front of him, he reiterates his point of view that there are issues they need to discuss. The desk head continues to ignore him, so he restates his position a second time. The desk head maintains her rude and uncooperative approach, but the auditor knows that right is on his side. He continues to state his requirements of her until she chooses to raise her head from her work and engage with him.

■ An executive coach is hired by a retail sales manager to coach his team of four saleswomen. She explains to him that she will maintain strict confidentiality agreements with each of the four people she coaches. However, she says that she is keen to work well with him too, so if he would like feedback of the progress on any of the coaching programs, she will provide it for him in the form of an update against program goals. She makes it clear that she will not speak about the content or process of individual coaching meetings with him. She then suggests that should he want more detailed feedback than she is able to provide him with given these parameters, he should speak directly with each of the four people himself. She makes the same agreement with each of the four clients, and begins work on their programs. Three weeks later the manager calls her, and asks for feedback on the psychometric tests that she has been using with the four members of the sales team. She refuses to give him the information, and reminds him of their previous conversation about her commitment to a clear ethical code. He says that he needs to know the outputs of the psychometric tests she has been administering for his human resources file. The coach doesn't quite believe him, but rather than say so directly, she suggests that he approach each of his team individually with his request for their psychometric feedback, and ends the call politely but firmly.

In each of these situations the main character has a clearly articulated and firmly held conviction about just where to draw the line. In each scenario the central character is able to retain influence and control in the situation by enforcing that line.

CLARIFYING THE BOUNDARIES

Let's examine the nature of the boundaries in each case.

The First Example

In the first case the boundary is the law of the land, which precludes unroadworthy vehicles from being driven on the roads. The mechanic gets paid to determine which vehicles are roadworthy and which are not. He also knows that his boss is as committed to upholding the law as he is, and will support him should he need his help. He knows from past experience that his boss will take the same line as him in cases where a vehicle is not roadworthy. Rather than be intimidated by his customer's manipulative comments about needing the car for his children, or his threat to go to his manager and complain about him, the mechanic stands his ground. He wants to enforce the law and perform his role well. In fact, when the car owner ups the stakes and threatens to complain about him to his boss, he welcomes the involvement of his manager, safe in the knowledge that he will come down on his side and respect the law too. Had his boss been a different character, one open to turning a blind eye, then the mechanic would have had to make a different choice. He would have had to decide whether he too would break the law and let an unsuitable car onto the road, or whether he would be prepared to stand up to his customer and his boss, and in the course of doing so, risk compromising his relationship with his manager and potentially place his job in jeopardy.

The Second Example

In the second instance the boundary is internal to the auditor, and it is also in his job description. It takes the form of his clear understanding that he is paid to safeguard the trading environment he is auditing even if his findings go against the wishes of the desk head in charge of that trading business. Even though the desk head is by far the more influential of the two of them in organizational terms, he believes that he is employed to carry out a specific function, and he takes his responsibility to his employer very seriously. He wants to do the right thing, and also knows that his job description and company policy require that he flag up risk factors in the trading environment. He stands up to the verbal intimidation, rudeness, and attempts to humiliate him employed by the trading desk head, because he wants to highlight key risks in her trading environment so that they can be addressed, and mitigated or eliminated. The influencing tactic he employs is to repeat his aim of discussing his findings with the desk head in the same level, firm tone until she engages with him. She learns that her tactics will not dissuade him from his course of action, and she eventually relents.

The Third Example

In the third instance the boundary is internal to the coach. It takes the form of an ethical commitment she has made to the clients with whom she works on coaching programs. She subscribes to a clearly articulated code of ethics that preclude her from speaking about the content of a coaching meeting outside of that meeting. She won't break this code of conduct even when the person paying her to do the work, the person who could throw her off the project, asks her to. When her client the sales manager calls her and asks her for the psychometric feedback, she is immediately on the alert and alive to his tactics. He is the person paying for her to carry out the work, and he could decide that, if she won't tell him what he wants to know, he will sack her. But she stands by her ethical standards and her promise to the people she is coaching. She has guaranteed each of them confidentiality, and refuses to tell their manager the results of their psychometric tests. Even when he tries a second time to pressurize her to give up the information, this time suggesting to her that it would be normal practice for the information she has to find its way onto a HR form he needs to complete, she isn't fooled. She sees through his manipulative ploy. She thinks his words are designed to throw her off guard and divulge the information she wishes to keep confidential. So she refers him to his team members before firmly but politely ending the call.

STANDING FIRM

In each of these three cases, while the specific dynamics are different, the challenge before the main character is essentially the same. Do they give in to pressure and do something that they don't want to do, or do they stick to their guns and stand firm in the face of opposition despite the risks? In each case the greatest influence that the main character can bring to bear in the situation is to stick to their sense of what is right and what is wrong. In each case their clear commitment to that boundary strengthens their will to stand firm, and prevents them from giving in to aggression, threats, and manipulation. It gives them influence in the situation, and enables each of them to stand up to pressure to behave in ways they know to be:

- Potentially hazardous to life.
- Illegal.
- Unethical.
- Or irresponsible.

Each of these situations is clear-cut. In each case the question of where to draw the line is very obvious. It is merely a question of the will of the main character, and it is not a difficult issue for someone with any integrity. Also, in each situation there will be very real consequences for the main character to deal with should they take the wrong option. The mechanic will get into trouble with the law and his boss should the vehicle's brakes fail and someone get hurt. The internal auditor will get into trouble with his boss and senior banking executives should the bank subsequently lose money because he allowed trading to continue in a trading environment he knew to be unsafe. If she divulges information given to her in a coaching meeting, the executive coach will lose the trust of her coaching clients, and gain a reputation as a coach who doesn't respect client confidentiality, both of which instances will likely lose her business and damage her credibility.

However, the primary motivation for each of these characters is not their fear of the potential consequences. It is their conviction that they want to do the right thing and act in accordance with their values and ethical frameworks. Crucially, each of them has developed the:

- Ability to stand their ground.
- Verbal dexterity to convey their determination to fight their corner.
- Strength of resolve to remain in the conversation until they attain an outcome they are comfortable with.

However, on some occasions the issues are not so unambiguous and the boundaries are less distinct. Sometimes the main character doesn't possess sufficient influencing ability to bring the conversation to a conclusion they consider satisfactory. And sometimes they need to influence their manager that his recent decision is both counter-productive and ill judged. Let's consider a longer example which is set in the retail sector.

CASE STUDY FIVE: TRADING UP

A hard-working retail store employee is asked to make the move up to store manager and run a store that is located in a shopping center on the outskirts of the city in which he lives. He is to replace a popular and effective store manager who had been employed in the role for 12 years. The store employee is delighted at the promotion and accepts the role. His new store sells a range of household, clothing, and garden lines, and has 26 members of staff. The newly promoted store manager reports to the sales director, who is based 80 miles away at the company's head office. What the store manager doesn't know is that the sales director is part of a competitive and sniping board, and that he expends a considerable amount of energy and time handling his peers in order to keep one step ahead of them.

The sales director prefers to communicate with his 20 store managers via email message or telephone call. Two weeks into his new role, the store manager receives a call from the sales director informing him that he must lose three members of staff. The sales director simply gives the store manager this news, and offers no rationale to account for the unwelcome turn of events. The store manager is unhappy at being given this directive, and protests. He says that his store will benefit from an ongoing facelift to the entire shopping center, and that he anticipates the new-look center will attract more customers, not fewer. Despite the fact that he makes his points passionately, his boss is unmoved. The sales director tells the store manager to go ahead with the redundancies, and the store manager is left with the distinct impression that his boss isn't interested in a dialogue about the situation. He seems only interested in telling the store manager what his decision is, before leaving him to implement it.

The store manager is a loyal man, and he finds the process of making three members of staff redundant very difficult indeed, even though he has only known the people involved for a short period of time. In the weeks that follow the redundancy notices, the facelift to the shopping center is completed and the store does do more business than in the previous few months. The remaining members of staff complain that they are rushed off their feet. The store manager decides to come in on Saturday afternoons, traditionally one of his days off, to help out.

He experiences his job as increasingly stressful. The sales director continues to call him and issue directives which he simply expects the store manager to implement. The store manager thinks that some of these directives are counter-productive, and likely to have an adverse impact on morale or customer service standards. During these calls the sales director is both high-handed and indifferent to any of the store manager's increasingly inadequate attempts to influence him towards a different point of view.

On one occasion the store manager receives a telephone call from the sales director, telling him that he has hired a firm of mystery shoppers who will be operating in all the stores over the next three months. The store manager is left in no doubt that the results of the mystery shopper campaign will be closely reviewed by the sales director. He tells his staff the news later in the day. He is embarrassed to do so, and feels that his employees will not welcome the news. In fact it is worse than that, as two of the more vocal members of staff take the use of mystery shoppers as a sign that the sales director thinks they are actually underperforming. Another asks why the money that is being 'wasted on gimmicks' can't be spent hiring more staff.

The store manager agrees with both points of view, but thinks it is his job to present the campaign as effectively as possible to his employees. He does a good job of selling the business benefits of the mystery shopper campaign to his staff. He also tells himself again that the sales director is under enormous pressure, and that while he finds his remote and task-focused style alien and unpredictable, his role is to support his manager's decisions, present them as best he can to his staff, and then implement them effectively. Two more experienced people resign over the following week, and both go to work for the supermarket at the other side of the shopping center. They are both replaced with less experienced people.

After two weeks of the mystery shopper campaign, and with sales revenue neither increasing nor decreasing, the store manager decides to try to influence the sales director that he needs additional staff. This telephone meeting goes less well than his previous calls with his boss. During the call the sales director is peremptory and short with the store manager. He tells him that everyone is under pressure, his job is to make savings and increase revenue, and there is no budget for additional staff. The store manager forms the view that the sales director is neither willing to understand the pressure his decisions place upon his staff, nor open to being influenced toward any view but his own. He doesn't sleep at all that night, and the following day he muddles up orders and sends the wrong payment to one of the store's suppliers. Then he snaps at two members of staff who come to talk to him, ordering them out of his office before he has heard what they came to say. That evening his partner suggests he resign before he becomes ill.

Over a period of a few months the store manager eventually comes to the view that his position at work is no longer tenable. After starting a row with his partner one weekend over something trivial, he decides that enough is enough. He resigns from his role, although with much guilt at leaving his team in the lurch.

The Opportunity to Influence

In this scenario a new store manager has to influence his new boss that he will be an able replacement for his predecessor. To achieve this outcome he needs to build influence with a sales director who is a poor communicator as well as being both unilateral and hard to influence. The stakes are high for the new store manager. If he fails to build influence with his autocratic boss over the central, early issue of redundancies, the store manager will find himself on the back foot from the very start of the relationship. He will find that the sales director assumes the right to run his store for him, and that he uses an increasingly directive and unsupportive style when dealing with him, denying him influence and reducing his views to trivial and irrelevant. Under these circumstances the store manager will find that he experiences a growing issue working for a man who reduces him to a minion, whom he considers to be there simply to carry out his orders whether or not he agrees with them. The store manager will lose his way in his job and his life, and will become stressed and unwell.

Handling the Personalities

Let's revisit the action from the start to identify the issues that prevent the store manager from building influence with his boss. We will also outline an influencing strategy which he could have used to encourage his manager to reconsider his decision to lay off three members of the store's workforce.

When his boss calls him and asks him to make three members of staff redundant, the store manager needs to see this for the red flag it is. He needs to stop and ask himself why redundancies were not discussed with him at the same time he was offered the new role. He needs to question what has happened in the intervening two weeks to justify taking action as drastic as making three of his employees redundant. He needs to find out what the context for this decision is, and get to the bottom of why it has been made. He needs to *understand* what is going on in the mind of the sales director that could possibly justify this course of action. He needs to make it a priority to get his boss to talk to him, find out what is going on, and listen to his feedback preparatory to putting an effective influencing argument to him. He needs to engage the sales director in a conversation about his aims and objectives in making people redundant. How the store manager interprets this influencing situation and responds to it will go a long way to defining the rest of his relationship with his new manager.

The store manager is right to object to the decision, and has a potentially decisive argument up his sleeve. Given the facelift to the shopping center, his store *could* reasonably expect to do more business in the coming months and not less. In this case the store will need to retain its current staff and possibly hire additional employees. It is particularly important for the store manager to use this issue effectively, and to put up an influential argument at this early point in his relationship with his manager. He needs to demonstrate to his boss that he can hold his own in a conversation with him, even when the sales director wishes to communicate a decision as a fait accompli and adopts a directive approach to the meeting. The point he makes is sound enough, but the problem lies with both the way in which he frames his point and the way in which articulates it.

Let's look at the way he frames his argument first. The store manager makes no attempt to understand his boss's decision before he makes his impassioned plea. He doesn't ask why his boss wants to take what, to him, appears to be an ill-thought-out and self-defeating course of action. He doesn't:

- Attempt to understand the pressures on the sales director that have led him to make this decision.
- Question him to understand the business case for the decision.
- Ask him to expand on the context surrounding the decision.
- Ask him what impact he thinks this decision might have on his store.

Instead he makes what sounds to the sales director an emotional petition, a petition which comes across to the sales director as an inexperienced store manager questioning his judgment and working against him. It has the direct effect of making the sales director more intransigent and less willing to participate further in the discussion.

Had the store manager asked the right questions in the right way, he would have understood that the sales director is under pressure from his board-level peers to increase profit margins across the retail outlets, and has decided that the quickest way to do this is to reduce costs. Armed with this information the store manager has a good chance of framing his key point in a way that will encourage the sales director to hear him, and at least consider reviewing his decision.

The store manager needs to respectfully suggest to the sales director that making people redundant may well be the right thing to do, but he'd like to talk it through with him. Then he can introduce his argument about the shopping center facelift, something about which the sales director, who is based 80 miles away, is probably unaware. He could suggest that the store's sales figures will likely increase over the next few months as more customers use the store. Then he can suggest that he retain all his staff in the short term, compare sales revenue figures for the three months after the facelift with sales revenue figures from the three months prior to the facelift, and let the sales director take a view at that time.

This approach is likely to influence the sales director because it:

- Addresses the real issue with which the sales director is grappling, that of how to increase profit in the stores.
- Leaves control of the decision-making process surrounding any potential redundancies with the sales director.
- Suggests that the decision about whether or not to make staff redundant will be made on the basis of clear data.
- Sets out a time frame for this decision.
- Is respectful to the position and status of the sales director.
- Is a clear business argument.
- Isn't a direct contradiction of a conclusion to which the sales director has already arrived.

This approach, one in which the store manager presents himself as respectful to his manager's position and working with him toward achieving his objectives, is much more likely to influence the sales director than a heart-felt plea about the fascia of the shopping center. The sales director will hear these arguments and will form the view that the store manager knows his own mind, is unlikely to cave in easily, and may well be helpful to him. He may not want to do an instant U-turn and tell the store manager in this call that he will amend his decision. He may want to go away and think about it before calling him back, but it is likely that these data-centric business-focused arguments will influence him. If sales revenue does increase over the next three months as the store manager predicts, then the figures will bear this out. Furthermore, these figures will be useful to the sales director, as he can present them at the relevant board meeting as further proof to his difficult peers of his value to the business.

However, the style with which the store manager handles this call is also important. He needs to step back from his own emotion and take a breath. Then he needs to adopt a calm, steady, and factual approach, one that mirrors the sales director's realistic and measured way of speaking. However, if all of these influencing tactics fail, and the sales director still expects the store manager to comply with his directive and make three people redundant, the store manager mustn't just submit. He needs to say that he doesn't agree with the decision and would rather not implement it, but that he will do so because it is the sales director's call. This preserves his integrity and makes it clear that he has a choice in the matter. It enables the store manager to end a challenging conversation on a note of mutual respect. It also gives the sales director the clear message that the store manager decides what the store manager will and will not do, and the sales director does not. However, the store manager doesn't manage to do any of these things, and despite having a valid and potentially compelling argument, he fails to influence his boss at all. From that moment onwards he is in trouble.

Let's now take a more detailed look at the characters of the sales director and store manager to understand the evolving dynamic between them.

The Sales Director

The sales director is a man whose preferred management style involves imposing his will on his managers – at least until he has worked with them long enough to allow them some latitude. He is a man who doesn't consult easily, rarely listens, and prefers to direct his staff rather than discuss issues with them. He often lays expectations upon them, whether or not they are comfortable with them, and at these times, simply expects compliance with his will. As such his primary frame of reference is his own wishes, and he prefers to listen to no other view on any subject.

The sales director is sufficiently removed from the day-to-day operation of the stores that he can make tough decisions without considering the true impact of his hard-nosed directives on the people affected by them. To him, making three members of staff redundant is a 'business decision' which carries no sentiment. It does not occur to him that his decision might appear ill-thought-out to the store manager who has to implement it, or his remaining staff who will have to pick up the slack. It doesn't occur to him that, without also communicating the context and rationale for his decision, he could appear out of touch and arbitrary. He doesn't consider such issues to be important. He makes this decision on the basis of financial considerations only, and considers that his view on the matter is sufficient.

However, all this said, he is open to being influenced provided that the right arguments are positioned with him in the right way. He will hear a suggestion which is positioned as being about *his* interests as opposed to the interests of the speaker. He will hear a suggestion pointing out in a low-key, sober style what the risks are in his proposals that he might want to consider, or identifying what opportunities he is overlooking in the situation, or suggesting a more effective way to meet his objectives. But, and this is key, the tone and manner of these suggestions needs to leave the sales director with no doubt at all that they are being made with *his* goals in mind, that they are being made to be helpful to *him*, and that they are being made to enable *him* to better achieve *his* aims. He needs to hear them as a service to *him* if he is to be influenced by them. He will not be influenced if he hears the suggestions as what he would think of as counter-proposals, disagreement, opposition, or dissent, or if he thinks that the colleague making the suggestion is doing so for their own purposes and not his. The wording and the style of delivery are crucial.

The Store Manager

The store manager is an amiable and good-natured man. He is hard working and no fool, but he has a fatal flaw. He is deferential to authority, even poor authority, and thinks that ultimately, it is his job to carry out the decisions of his boss. While he will have his say and give a view early on in a conversation, if he thinks that his opinion is not wanted he desists straight away.

On these occasions he doesn't persevere and make it his job to get the sales director to hear him. He conserves his energy, thinking that it will be better to do what the sales director wants, rather than risk an argument with his boss. It is this lack of resolve that undermines him, leaving him unable to draw the line or build influence with his manager. While it is true that he cannot easily refuse to implement a decision made by someone with more seniority than him without suffering some consequences, it is also true that failing to stand up for what he believes to be right won't do him any good either.

His style of opting out of contentious discussions early on leaves him with few options when working with a boss who spends most of his time covering his back with his board-level peers, and who doesn't want, as he would see it, to waste time he hasn't got discussing issues with his store managers. The store manager fails to find a balance that enables him to put his point across and stand by his own values sufficiently that he can choose to defer to the will of his boss should his argument prove ineffective. Instead he simply gives in, early and without a fight.

The Challenge Facing the Store Manager

So, once he has failed in his first attempt to influence his boss, the question before the store manager is: does he want to continue to use his current ineffective influencing style and risk becoming powerless in his relationship with his boss, or does he want to develop his influencing skills and strengthen his resolve so that he stands some chance of holding his own with the sales director?

To achieve the latter option he must be prepared to stop deferring to unsound leadership, work hard to understand his boss, and find ways of framing his input to influencing conversations so that his boss perceives it to be useful to him. He must:

- Make and keep clear commitments to himself about where to draw the line when he disagrees with his boss. He needs to decide which issues he must push back on and which he can afford to concede. These boundaries will primarily take the form of clarity in his own mind about at what point he needs to contest his boss's directives, and when he can afford to let a directive go.
- Develop a suite of effective influencing skills. Simply giving his impassioned views or beliefs on a situation won't do it. He needs to initiate and sustain effective influencing conversations with his manager on all the points he feels strongly about, and if need be, be prepared to finally say no.

If he doesn't do these things, then the sales director will continue to see the store manager as a compliant and amenable person. He will regard him as someone who, while he may have a clear sense of where he wants to draw the line, doesn't have the skills to enable him to actually do so. The sales director will continue to direct him and deny him influence, and the store manager will end up feeling powerless in his relationship with his boss, and possibly in his own store as well.

The Outcome

Sadly for him, the store manager fails to build influence with his boss after their first crucial conversation about redundancies. He continues to make the same mistakes when dealing with his boss, and his boss continues to issue him with directives which the store manager then implements, often against his better judgment. Even when right and common sense are on his side, he fails to bring any influence to bear with his manager.

His quality of life deteriorates, and after he starts to make mistakes at work and behaves unreasonably towards his staff, he eventually snaps at home. This is the point at which he decides that enough is enough. He resigns, although with considerable guilt that he has left his staff to the whims of the sales director.

Conclusions

In this situation the directive and unsupportive management style of a boss, coupled with the failure of the store manager to set and keep clear boundaries with him, or to frame his views effectively when seeking to influence him, eventually create an untenable situation for the store manager. Instead of working to understand the sales director's decisions, frame his points around his boss's objectives, and adopt a style which, however unnatural for him, proves influential with his boss, the store manager takes a wrong turn early on, and simply complies with his boss's wishes out of a mistaken sense of duty. His relationship with himself is just as much the issue for this store manager as is his relationship with his boss. The more he thinks 'I must support my boss,' or 'I must step up to the plate,' or 'I must act responsibly toward my employer,' the more he sells himself short. In order to build any influence in a difficult situation, he needs to retain control of his own boundaries, work hard to influence his boss, and be prepared to draw the line clearly and firmly whenever he thinks his boss's decisions will injure his store, his staff, or his customers.

YOUR INFLUENCING BEHAVIOR

We have just examined an example in which a hard-working but unwise manager fails to build influence with his directive boss and ends up implementing a series of decisions he does not agree with. You may now like to consider a situation from your working life. Identify a situation in which you were asked by a peer or a manager to implement a decision or take a course of action that did not sit comfortably with you. Bring the situation to mind and then answer the following questions about it. You can jot down your answers to each of the questions in the space below it:

■ Thinking about that specific situation, what were you asked to do and what was your initial reaction on being asked to take that course of action?

■ What influencing argument did you use to convey your views at the time? To what extent was this argument successful?

■ Where did you want to draw the line? How effective were you at communicating this boundary to your colleague?

■ Should you find yourself in the same situation again, what would you do differently so that you have a better chance of building influence with your colleague?

This case study concerned a situation in which it is vital for an employee to find a way of influencing his boss over whether or not to make staff redundant, at a time when his store could reasonably have expected to do more business rather than less. The issue is complicated for him by the fact that he is new into the role and unfamiliar with his new boss. Let's now consider a different situation, one in which you have said firmly and clearly that you won't cross a particular line, but your senior colleague, someone you know more from a distance, simply refuses to take no for an answer, and requires you to cross it anyway. Consider the following case study, which is set in a consultancy firm.

CASE STUDY SIX: UNDUE PRESSURE

A senior partner in the business services team of a large multinational consultancy firm makes a mistake, and omits including a sizable piece of business in the budget for his project with his major client. He decides that he cannot afford to lose face by going back to his client at this late stage and asking for more money, so he determines to ask one of the more junior consultants in the forensic team to do the work for free. The benefit to him of this approach is that his client will get the full service as outlined in his proposal, and he won't have to admit to his client or his colleagues that he has under-billed for the work.

He contacts the junior colleague from the forensic team whom he has selected to do the work, and arranges a meeting with him, telling him that he has something for him to do. The junior consultant is delighted that the senior partner from another department wants to work with him. He knows his partner sufficiently to say hello to him, but has not worked with him before. Without being clear what precisely the work will entail, the consultant takes it as a pat on the back that the partner wants to work with him, and looks forward to the meeting. He listens to his senior colleague's plans for him, and quickly moves from surprise to dismay. He realizes that his more experienced colleague has singled him out for special attention because he believes that he will do a good job, but that he will do it for free *and* put the work to the top of his priority list. He starts to protest, but is silenced by an authoritative command from the senior figure, who informs him that it would be in his best interests to oblige him.

The consultant feels trapped. On the one hand he doesn't want to alienate this powerful and influential figure. On the other hand he doesn't think it is right that he is being asked to drop all his current fee-earning work for a piece of non-fee-earning work, a piece of work that he is being asked to do for clients he doesn't know on behalf of another department in his firm. There are a number of ways in which he could respond to this situation. Let's explore three of them:

■ The junior consultant decides to influence the partner through an appeal to his better nature, and thinks that the best way to do this is to point out the obvious injustice of his proposals. He takes a deep breath and explains that he has a heavy workload that precludes him from taking on additional work at that juncture. He says that he thinks it is unfair of the partner to ask him to relegate his own fee-earning work for work that will not earn his department any money. He is astonished that the partner simply reiterates his requirement that the consultant undertake the work. He says that 'It is for the good of the firm,' and tells the consultant that he is sure he will enjoy it and learn from the experience. He then says, 'Is there anything else you wish to discuss?' before standing up and walking smartly out of the room without giving the consultant any time to reply.

- The junior consultant decides to influence the partner through an appeal to his client-centered values. He points out that, if he takes on the additional work, he will be letting his own clients down. He says he is sure that the partner wouldn't want the reputation of the firm to be affected by his inability to deliver because he has been taken off his current projects and put onto other work. The partner says in a smooth and commanding tone that people of his stature within the firm build its reputation with clients, and that the consultant shouldn't worry himself over things that don't concern him. He then tells him that he will send the relevant files over to him by the end of the morning, and leaves the room.

- The junior consultant decides that if he is to build any influence in this tricky situation he will have to play it quite carefully. He tells the partner that he would like to help him, and that the work sounds interesting. Then, without pausing in his delivery, he says that he must involve his department's partner in the discussions, so that the two partners can decide between them what would constitute the best way forward for the firm. When the partner replies with the words, 'That won't be necessary,' he consultant simply tells him that he would not be able to justify the absence of fees for the proposed work to his boss, and would prefer to square things off up front. He then stands up, says goodbye politely, and leaves the room. He returns to his desk and drafts an email which he sends to the forensic team partner and copies to the business services partner. He calls the forensic team partner's PA and asks her to draw his attention to the email as a matter of urgency. Then he gets back to his work.

The Opportunity to Influence

In this case study a senior partner tries to intimidate a consultant from another department into doing work for his client for free. The consultant has to find a way to influence the partner that he cannot do the work, but has to do so without upsetting him or causing him to become fractious and unpleasant. If he is unable to influence his more senior colleague that it is unreasonable of him to expect something for nothing from someone who doesn't even work for him, he may well find that he:

- Can't get out of the commitment.
- Gets into trouble with his own boss.
- Lets down his own clients.
- Paves the way for the partner to try a similar stunt again in the future.

However, if he alienates the influential partner he will also be in trouble. The partner may well find all sorts of ways to injure the reputation of his more junior colleague, or to deny him interesting opportunities in the future.

Handling the Personalities

Let's explore the three instances to examine how the consultant handles his more senior colleague.

The First Instance

In the first instance the consultant tries to influence the partner by appealing to his better nature. He makes a fundamental mistake in taking this line, because the partner doesn't really have a better nature. He has already demonstrated himself as someone unscrupulous enough to ask a more junior colleague to do work for free: worse, this is a colleague who doesn't report to him and who might feel intimidated by his seniority. The partner responds to the influencing arguments put to him about fairness and justice by sweeping them aside. He tries to embarrass the consultant into doing his will, and asks him to take a course of action he quite rightly objects to by saying 'It is for the good of the firm.' This is quite clearly only true from a certain perspective: his own. It is not in the best interests of the firm to do work that it doesn't bill for. Nor is it in the best interests of the firm to remove one of its consultants from fee-earning work for one client in order for him to carry out alternative work for another client, if doing so means that he will fail his first client. And, in this case, that is exactly what will happen. The consultant shoots himself in the foot by not seeing the partner's duplicity for what it is, and by using an inadequate and ineffective influencing argument with him. He suffers the indignity of watching the partner sweep out of the office, after having asked him a question to which he does not want to reply.

The Second Instance

In the second instance the consultant tries to influence the partner by pointing out the pitfalls for the firm if he does as he is asked. He says, reasonably enough, that he cannot carry out two projects at once, and if he works for the partner's clients, he will let down his own. He says this will injure the reputation of the firm. Unfortunately for him, this argument doesn't work either. It merely gives the unprincipled partner more ammunition with which to compete back. He patronizes his junior colleague telling him that it is people like *him* who build the reputation of the firm, and that he shouldn't be worrying about issues that he cannot influence. The partner ruthlessly puts his junior colleague in his place for daring to question his judgment over client-facing issues, and leaves him in no doubt that he holds the trump cards. He seizes the moment and tells the consultant that he will send the relevant files over to him. The consultant is defeated, and may well feel compelled to attend to the work for fear of the consequences if he doesn't.

The Third Instance

In the third instance the consultant selects an influencing strategy that is judicious and effective. He decides to step out of the decision-making process about whether he should or should not take on the additional work and refer the matter upwards. This works because it makes the partner aware that the ramifications of his illicit proposal to the consultant affect more than the consultant himself. They also affect his boss, the forensic partner. By bringing this senior figure into the argument, the consultant demonstrates that he is more than a match for the business services partner. He takes control of the meeting by telling the partner that he would like to do the work but really needs to sign it off with his own partner. He knows full well that his partner, indeed any partner, would take a dim view of one of their peers tapping up one of his team members to do work for free for their department's client. The consultant isn't thrown by the partner's hasty 'That won't be necessary,' and simply reiterates his view that it would be better to involve his partner at an early stage. He then leaves the room and documents everything in an email straightaway so that the business services partner cannot easily maneuver behind the scenes.

Then he gets back to his work and lets the two senior peers sort it out.

The Outcome

Only in the third instance is the consultant able to bring any influence to bear in this tricky situation. In the first two instances he quickly finds that he has no influence at all in the situation, even though what the partner is requesting of him is obviously unfair and unreasonable. However, as soon as the consultant brings his own partner into the discussion, he is able to influence the outcome. Why does this tactic work? It works because it means that the partner will have to deal with someone of equal organizational standing to him, and therefore will not be able simply to impose his will on the situation. He knows that the forensic partner will not be at all pleased with his proposals, and will most likely oppose them, or only allow them on condition that he gets something back in exchange. The consultant will still have to deal with a potentially unpleasant backlash from the business services partner should he decide to make life difficult for him, but he has protected himself from undertaking work that isn't his to do, for which he will get no credit, that will result in his letting down his own client, and that will likely get him into trouble with his own boss.

Conclusions

There are times when staying in the conversation and fighting your corner is the most influential thing to do. There are also times when the most influence that can be brought to bear in a situation involves stepping out of the discussion and letting someone more senior resolve it. This is the case in this scenario. Whatever influencing arguments the consultant uses will be trumped by the partner. He is, for some reason of his own, minded to ask a junior employee at his firm to leave his own work and do something for him for free. He is a competitive and corrupt character, and quite willing to throw his weight around. He will not be persuaded by arguments about client expectations or workload, or the unfairness of the request. He is not concerned with any of these issues. He is only concerned with getting his own way. The best way to limit his excesses and prevent him from imposing his will on the situation is to match him seniority for seniority. This is the line that the consultant takes in the third instance, and he is successful at influencing a situation which otherwise threatens to become uncomfortable for him.

YOUR INFLUENCING BEHAVIOR

The previous example focuses on how a more junior colleague resists pressure to act in ways he objects to when asked to do so by a more senior figure in his firm. You might like to apply the material to your own working life. Bring a specific situation to mind in which a senior colleague asked you to take action you didn't want to take, then answer the following questions. You can jot down your answers to each of the questions in the space below it:

■ Thinking about that specific situation, which senior colleague asked you to do what? Why did this colleague want you to act in this way?

■ What made you uncomfortable about this situation?

■ How did you position your objections with your colleague?

■ How effective did this influencing strategy prove to be? In what ways did it prove to be ineffective?

■ Should you need to handle a similar situation in the future, what changes will you make to your influencing strategy so that it proves more decisive?

SUMMARY AND NEXT CHAPTER

This chapter focused on how to build influence in a situation where you are asked to take a course of action that conflicts with your values or that you think is counter-productive to your work or team. It:

■ Suggested that for most of you, most of the time, the ethical boundaries around your work will be unambiguous.
■ Suggested that most of the time you will need to try and resolve issues person to person with your colleague at the time they raise them with you.
■ Proposed that in some situations appealing to a higher authority is the best way to influence a situation where you are outmatched and losing.
■ Illustrated that committing to these boundaries is a question of both your will and your levels of skill at remaining in an influencing conversation long enough to bring it to a satisfactory conclusion.

- Examined how important it is to make it a priority to build influence with a boss whose style does not sit comfortably with you.
- Highlighted the crucial importance of framing your input around the issues that matter to your boss when seeking to overturn a decision you disagree with.
- Examined a range of responses you could make to a senior member of your organization who wants you to take a course of action that is both unreasonable and unfair.
- Highlighted how being clear in your own mind about where to draw the line is crucial if you are to stand your ground when under pressure from a colleague.
- Included an opportunity for you to apply the material to your working life.

The next chapter explores how to retain the influence that you have already worked hard to build in situations when things are going well for you, and in situations when they are not.

CHAPTER 6

Retaining Influence, Adding Value

Things are going well for you. You have worked hard to build influence with the key people with whom you need to work productively day in, day out. You have established effective relationships with members of your team, with your peer group, and with the senior managers with whom you need to work. Most of the time you are able to get done the things you need to do to perform effectively in your role, and when you cannot find a way forward with a particular colleague, you can in the main engage in a discussion with them around the issues to find a way forward. However, you are aware that you cannot take the influence you have gained for granted. You respect the fact that retaining influence requires just as much thought, application, and skill as gaining it in the first place.

This chapter will focus on how to retain influence with key workplace contacts, making sure that your input consistently adds value to discussions, debates, and decision-making processes. It will explore how to maintain influence over a period of time when things continue to go well for you, as well as when they don't and your reputation is called into question. The chapter will address the issues involved in choosing to compromise to keep a relationship – and your influence in it – viable, and knowing how to step back from the political landscape and assess how the changing priorities of your senior managers will affect you and your relationships with them in the future.

The chapter will highlight skills to help you retain influence in good times and in bad. It will help you to step back from your key workplace relationships and:

■ Clarify a range of tactics that you could use to help you sustain influence with your colleagues in the long term.
■ Give yourself the best chance of acting in effective and influential ways should you find that you are called on to act carefully in defense of your reputation.
■ Recognize what you might need to do to retain influence with a key colleague as their priorities and expectations of you change over time.

THE ROLE OF FACT AND YOUR OPINION IN RETAINING INFLUENCE

Let's set the scene by exploring the role of fact and your opinion in retaining influence. We will explore the situation in which you have already acquired a degree of influence and want to build on it by putting forward a new idea. Clearly, what you say and how you say it is an important part of your ongoing contribution to your organization, and a key component in gaining and subsequently sustaining influence with your colleagues. Deciding:

■   When to give an opinion.
■   To whom.
■   And over what is a key, learned skill.

So is deciding when to be quiet, when to listen, when to ask questions, and when to clarify a colleague's verbal contribution, perhaps making a distinction between what is a fact and what is a perception. Those of you who are skilled at contributing verbally at work will understand that you can gain significant influence – and credibility – by judiciously combining:

■   A factual analysis of the issues under discussion

With:

■   Your opinion about the way forward given those facts.

Let's establish these principles by considering the following two short examples:

■   A small firm of independent financial advisors is going through a difficult patch and needs to make some savings. The business owner tells his staff of six people that he wants them to put forward cost-reduction ideas, none of which are to include making anyone redundant. He receives a number of suggestions, and arranges a meeting of the entire staff at which to discuss the ins and outs of the various ideas.

   The meeting quickly gets bogged down with different people putting forward the merits of their own ideas. Little progress is made, and as the meeting progresses it becomes less clear which ideas from the several on the table represent the best options for the firm. The meeting descends into suggestions, counter-suggestions, and a degree of argument about which ideas to support and which to jettison, with most people becoming entrenched in support of their own proposals.

The office manager is one of the people to submit an idea. She proposes buying a projector, screen, and laptop for the in-house presentations that the firm makes to its clients. At present the company hires the relevant equipment by the hour from a local production company. The office manager has a sound reputation around the firm. In advance of the meeting she prepares some figures to back up her case. She compares the costs of hiring the equipment over the past two years with the investment required to buy and install both new and secondhand kit. She waits for a lull in the debate and then puts forward her idea, outlining her view that it would be more cost-efficient in the long run to purchase the equipment than to continue to hire it from the production company. She makes a compelling case, combining her factual analysis of the costs with her view about the monetary savings, efficiency, and timesavings involved in the firm owning its own equipment. The business owner gives her the go-ahead as soon as she outlines her suggestion, without waiting for a debate about its merits to develop. He is impressed at her proactive and responsible approach to the company's finances, and makes a mental note to involve her in future purchasing decisions.

■ An editor in a European travel-writing publisher wants to commission a new series of books. The books will be written by people who have moved from one European country to another to start a business, and then traveled extensively in the country to which they have relocated. Her intuitive sense is that there will be a ready market for the books among the increasing number of people moving between EU countries. She has a positive reputation with her publishing director, with whom she has worked for three years, and decides to make an appointment with her to discuss the idea. But, aware that her peers and more junior colleagues regularly put ideas to their boss, she changes her mind and decides to do some research in advance of the meeting, research aimed at proving her case.

Several weeks later she approaches the publishing director with a well-crafted presentation of her idea. She outlines in detail the number and type of businesses relocating from one European country to another, before describing the main issues they face once they have settled. She then repositions the series of books so that it appeals to the non-working members of the emigrant family – spouses, children, and dependent relatives – who are more likely to want to travel around the country to which they have moved than the income generators in the family. The publishing director is open to the idea, and gives the editor the go-ahead to approach potential writers for the first six books. She comments that the evidence to support the series proposal had been decisive in convincing her of the merits of the idea.

In both of these examples the personal opinion of the main character in and of itself, no matter how sound, will not be enough to secure them the outcome they want. Even though both the main characters have good instincts and a positive reputation in their place of work, they recognize that they need to find a compelling factual reason to support their opinion before they can make a robust presentation to their boss. Without a factual context against which to establish their case, their personal opinion might appear either ill-thought-out or whimsical, even in a situation in which they actually do have something worth listening to.

The temptation for either character could have been to decide that *their reputation alone ought to be* enough to carry the day. But both characters realize at the start of the influencing process that they need to find some data to support their case, so that they can present their proposition as a judicious mixture of factual analysis and considered opinion. In both cases, this approach is successful in enabling a good idea to be taken forward. It results in the character originating the idea retaining a high level of influence with a key decision maker, and means that both of the main characters avoid the discomfort of being seen as employees who:

- Don't do the hard work preparatory to making suggestions.
- Take shortcuts instead.
- Don't think things through properly.
- Have their judgment questioned.

These examples illustrate that a combination of a factual presentation allied to your view of the way forward given those facts can prove especially decisive when your colleagues become bogged down arguing the rights and wrongs of different interpretations of the situation, or the merits and demerits of different possible strategies for addressing them. In these cases adding your own opinion to the mix will only serve to increase the likelihood of the argument becoming a battle of wills over whose opinion is more valid. Moving the discussion onto an analysis of the facts, preparatory to giving a view on those facts, can cut through the fog and produce progress. In this case it is your ability to:

■ Select salient facts.
■ Present them in a cogent way.
■ Deliver a succinct analysis of the implications of those facts.
■ Give a well-thought-out view about what you think needs to happen next, which will more often than not carry the day.

Using this combination of factual analysis and personal opinion can bring you credibility and respect. It can enhance your reputation as someone with sound judgment on complex issues, someone with sufficient confidence and clarity about those issues that they are prepared to present themselves as a professional advisor to their colleagues. When things are going well for you, when you need to set direction, or when you want to identify the key issues among a confusing mixture of perceptions, suggestions, and possibilities, these can be key skills to employ.

WHEN OPINION IS NOT ENOUGH

But what happens when things go wrong for you and you can no longer expect people to be swayed by your opinion – even an opinion volunteered in the context of salient facts – because it is your opinion that is being called into question? What happens when you cannot use the two tools which you normally rely on – your understanding of a situation and your opinion about that situation – and you have to use other tactics and skills instead? How do you turn around a situation that you cannot afford to let slip because of the reputational damage you will inevitably suffer if it does? Consider the following example, which is set in a design team of ten people in an investment bank.

A well-qualified and experienced designer joins the in-house team at an investment bank and spends six months developing her reputation with her colleagues. She is prompt to suggest new ideas, proactive in taking assignments, and makes astute observations about ways in which the team could work more effectively with the other departments in the bank. She establishes liking and respect with her colleagues, and gains a reputation for being engaged, knowledgeable, and reliable. After six months the head of the design team suggests that she build on the influence she has gained around the office and take on an additional role alongside her design work. He suggests that she manage the team's office move to the second floor.

The design team member is actually quite pleased to be offered this opportunity, and accepts. She sees it as a sign of her manager's good faith in her work to date, and her organization and project management skills. She begins her work, and enjoys the challenge of planning and implementing the office move. Initially she makes sure that she keeps a balance between her design work and managing the office move, but as she begins to realize the complexity of the work involved in relocating the office, she spends more and more time on that project. The responsibility of the office move weighs heavily on her shoulders, and she begins to neglect her design work, becomes inattentive at team meetings, and makes a number of errors. On three occasions she gives wrong information to her colleagues, information that they subsequently use in their work. On two of these occasions it is an internal coaching client who corrects the error, leaving her design team colleague looking foolish and feeling angry with her.

Feeling justified in her own mind because she is working flat out, the design team member doesn't address any of these issues with her colleagues when she hears about them. Even when attitudes towards her change around the office, and her colleagues start to ask her pointed questions about her work priorities, she makes a joke, convinced in her own mind that they must see how hard she is working. At this point the team manager steps in and asks to see her.

The design team member walks into her manager's office. She realizes that she is being called to account, and will need to use the meeting to explain her recent errors. There are a number of ways in which she could approach the meeting. Let's examine three of them:

■ The design team member pre-empts her manager's opening statements by asserting that she has been working flat out and is making good progress on the office move. She says that she is carrying a significant weight of responsibility, and knows that she has made a few minor mistakes recently. She asserts that she is going to crack on over the next few weeks, and once the office move is ready for implementation, she will be able to focus

fully again on her design work. She is discomfited to note that
her boss's expression remains impassive and unimpressed during
this speech, and that when she finishes speaking, he says, 'That
won't do.'

■ The design team member sits down facing her boss and waits for
him to speak. He tells her that he is concerned that a number of
errors have crept into her work, and that she hasn't taken any
obvious steps to address the consequences of these errors for the
colleagues who are relying on her. The design team member says
that she is well aware that she made a few errors recently, but
makes the point that she is working very hard. She continues
by saying that she does have it in mind to go and talk to the
colleagues involved and smooth things over with them. In the
pause which follows, she offers to do so straight away, and leaves
her manager's office, relieved to have kept the meeting so short.

■ The design team member says that she thinks the meeting is
likely to focus on her recent performance. She watches her boss
nod, then seizes the initiative. She tells him in a factual tone that
she has not left the office before 7 pm for each of the last eight
working days. She says that she has had only half an hour for
lunch on six of those days, and starts work before 8.30 every
morning. Then she says that, in giving him these facts, she is not
complaining, merely setting the scene. She tells her boss that she
is handling a complex project which involves moving 11 work
stations, 11 sets of filing systems and 11 people to a new location,
and that it is taking longer than she, and she suspects he, had
expected. She says that, while it pains her to make mistakes
in her design work, she is unable to carry out both the office
move preparations and her normal duties because of the size
of the moving project. She says she is aware her colleagues are
disappointed that she has made mistakes recently, and that she
would like an opportunity to set the record straight with them
at the next team meeting. She says she would like to fill them
in on how much work is involved in the office move project,
and explain the timescales she is working to in completing it.
She ends by saying that while she wants to complete a project
she has started, she does not want to do so at the expense of
her normal day-to-day work, and would like to make sure that
her reputation doesn't become too tarnished around the office.
She is relieved to hear her boss agree to give her a ten-minute
opening at the next team meeting.

In this situation the design team member has only a few minutes to handle a tricky meeting with her boss in a way which preserves her reputation and influence with him. Clearly he is discomforted enough by her recent errors and her general conduct around the office to call her to account. If she mishandles this meeting and loses his positive regard, on top of annoying her teammates, she could be in for a rough ride. She has to judge the mood of the meeting well, start it in the right place, and demonstrate sufficient understanding of the situation she has placed herself, her boss, and the team in if she is to retain influence with him. Let's revisit the three instances to identify the key differences between the ways in which she handles the meetings.

The First Instance

In the first instance the design team member gets it all wrong. She jumps in straight away without waiting for her boss to speak, and so gives herself no opportunity to judge his mood or the tone he wants to set for the meeting. She is instantly on the defensive, trying to justify her recent errors, and putting forward the view that she is working very hard indeed. She thinks that her, as she sees it, hard work is justification enough for her errors. She only looks at the situation from her own perspective, her own point of view, and ignores the issues that her errors have created for her colleagues and clients. Worse still, she makes the assumption that her opinion on the situation will be enough to influence her boss that she isn't really worthy of the reprimand she fears is coming. She relies on her point of view in the meeting, because her opinion has always been enough to influence her boss in the past.

But the context for this conversation is not the same as the context for previous meetings between her and her boss. Previously she has handled her work well. Now she is being called to account. Her boss is annoyed at what he sees as her slapdash approach, and he is not persuaded by her analysis of how hard she is working and how much responsibility she is carrying. He does not see these things as sufficient justification for her letting down her colleagues and clients. True, he may not have known just how much work is involved in the office move when he assigned the work to her, and he may be unaware of just how much pressure she is under, with too much to accomplish in each day. But, unless she explains the ins and outs of these things to him in sufficient detail that he can make up his own mind about the scope of the work she is undertaking, she will find that his view of her is unaltered. In fact, he hears her point of view on how hard she is working as further proof of her irresponsibility towards her colleagues, and tells her that her excuses aren't good enough. She is now in a worse position than she was in at the start of the meeting, when had she used a more effective approach, she would have stood a good chance of influencing him to change his view of her.

The Second Instance

In the second instance the design team member makes a good start to the meeting. She lets her boss speak first, and when he says that he is concerned at the number of mistakes she has been making recently, she addresses his point directly. She tells him that she realizes that her mistakes have put her colleagues in a difficult position, and offers to go straight away and smooth things over. In doing this she placates her boss, but crucially she misses the opportunity to influence him toward the view that, given her current workload and level of responsibility, it is inevitable that some things will slip. While he is relieved that she wants to make amends with her colleagues, her boss still does not know the true situation that the design team member is working in. He leaves the meeting with the same view he had when he came into it: that she is handling her responsibilities less effectively than he would like her to, and has let her standards slip. She may have placated his ire, but she hasn't influenced his view about her current conduct.

The Third Instance

In the third instance the design team member does a good job of giving her boss the factual information he needs to make up his own mind that she has too much to do. She brings sufficient influence to bear in the meeting that he agrees to work with her to repair the damage that has been done to her relationships with his colleagues, and while he doesn't say so directly to her, he does amend his view of her. She does this by giving him facts only. She doesn't complain, say she is working flat out, or excuse her mistakes on the basis of her workload. She merely tells him how long she has spent in the office in recent weeks, acknowledges the awkward situation her mistakes have created for her colleagues, and lets him fill in the blanks. He realizes that she has too much to do, and recognizes that despite this fact she is shouldering her responsibilities fully, even to the point of wanting to speak to her teammates at the next team meeting in order to set the record straight. He will be impressed with her hard work and commitment, and her ability to take the steps she wants to take without complaining or seeking to minimize the situation her errors have created. He now knows something about her that he didn't know before: that she can demonstrate a commendable degree of maturity when things go wrong for her.

LETTING THE FACTS SPEAK FOR THEMSELVES

This example illustrates the pitfalls of relying on your opinion to speak in your defense when it is your very opinion that is called into question. In this situation, one in which your judgment or conduct is called to account, offering justifications or explanation for your mistakes, or views about why they have happened, won't do it. Worse still, expecting your colleagues to be satisfied with your opinion that you are, for instance, working extra hard will leave you without influence in the situation, and could leave you looking as if you don't understand the issues you have created and don't have any answers to the points being put to you. You may well find that, no matter how true it is that you are working hard – or traveling a lot, or whatever the specific set of circumstances is – your colleagues will not be convinced, and will continue to doubt you, and retain questions in their minds about your performance, dedication, judgment, or commitment and effort.

A better route to take is that of giving your colleagues the facts they need to know to *make up their own mind* about you, and so form their own opinion about the situation you find yourself in. The influence you bring to bear by using this tactic is understated but powerful: you give your colleague the key facts they need, and trust them to come to a right conclusion about you and your situation, in order to buy yourself room to maneuver. Of course, you must use that room wisely, and take genuine steps to make good the relationships that have been adversely affected by your errors. But you should be able to move on with your reputation either intact or less damaged than it may prove to be should you rely on your erstwhile effective tactic of giving an opinion. Having regained the trust of your colleagues over time, you can then go back to giving an opinion. But, while your reputation is open to speculation, don't take the risk. Let the facts speak for themselves instead.

YOUR INFLUENCING BEHAVIOR

You may now like to identify a situation in which your reputation was called into question. Maybe you made a mistake, your view on a matter was suspect, or a decision you made proved to be a misjudgment. Bring a specific situation to mind, then answer the following questions about it. You can jot down your answers to each of the questions in the space below it:

■ Thinking about that specific situation, what did you say or do that brought your reputation into question?

■ Who called you to account over this issue, and in what way did they do so?

■ How did you respond to these points at the time? What key facts did you emphasize when addressing the points put to you?

■ To what extent did you rely on your opinion when stating your case? To what extent was this tactic effective?

■ What changes would you make to the way you handled this conversation should you have the opportunity to hold it again?

Having examined an example of where you needed to act judiciously to retain influence with your colleagues, let's now turn our attention to a different situation. This situation is one in which you recognize that the factors that brought you influence with your senior colleagues previously won't prove as influential with them in the future. Their priorities have changed, and consequently so have their expectations of you. Let's examine the issues by taking a look at a longer example, which is set in the technology group of a medium-sized accountancy firm.

CASE STUDY SEVEN: CHANGING PRIORITIES

The head of technology in a busy accountancy firm has an excellent reputation with the partners to whom he reports. He has worked effectively in his role for just over three years, and during that time he has established liking and respect with the senior team, who see him as reliable and hard-working. They regularly include him in a section of the monthly partners' meeting that focuses on identifying performance improvements that will increase the firm's ability to retain clients and provide them with higher standards of service.

The head of technology enjoys this role. It enables him to discuss ways in which technological improvements can play a part in improving service delivery to clients, which in turn enables him to build influence with the partners. Outside of the partners' meeting he makes it his business to approach them with new ideas about incremental technology changes that he would like them to consider, including changes to the software or hardware that he believes will add value to the firm's offer to its clients.

The partners are a small group of dedicated, steadfast men and women. They are sober and serious in demeanor. They respond well to the consistent, task-focused style of the head of technology. They like him and listen to his ideas. They don't always adopt them but they do always consider them. In turn, the technology head likes playing a part in determining the future direction of the firm, and enjoys the kudos and satisfaction that this role provides him with. Over a three-year period the head of technology builds sufficient influence with the partners that they, like him, come to see the firm's technology capability as central to its offer to clients. Towards the end of the second year of his employment he develops plans to undertake a major overhaul of the system, which aims to upgrade the range and quality of the firm's services to clients. After three years, they are half-way through the first of two phases of these plans.

But four months later the accountancy firm's fortunes take a turn for the worse, as a recession starts to hit the economy. Its business is affected, as several smaller clients leave to handle their own finances, and then two of its three biggest clients decide to change accountants. There is talk of redundancies around the firm as the ongoing recession creates further uncertainty in the economy. The head of technology notices that morale in his team has gone down, and worries when the more experienced members of his staff ask him what news he has for them. He doesn't have any.

The head of technology is a loyal man, and he is torn. On the one hand he would like to offer his team some information about how the partners are planning to handle potential redundancies, but on the other hand he recognizes that any questions from him on the subject may be precipitate or unwelcome. He realizes that he has been excluded from the last partners' meeting, a meeting that he would certainly have been asked to attend in better times. The technology manager doesn't want to let his team down by failing to supply them with any available information on potential redundancies, but equally he doesn't think that it would be timely or wise for him to approach any of the partners directly for specific information about his team's future. He tells his team that he is committed to selling the benefits of the entire technology team to the partners, and is actively looking for an opportunity to do so.

One afternoon he receives a call from one of the partners. The partner invites him to the following day's partners' meeting, and volunteers the information that decisions have yet to be made regarding redundancies. The technology head accepts the invitation, and sits down to plan for the meeting. Clearly there are issues that the partners want to speak with him about. Clearly he also has an opportunity to influence the partners. He knows that the role he has played at previous partners' meetings is no longer relevant to his attendance at this meeting: the context for his attendance at this meeting is not the same as the context for his attendance at previous partners' meetings. He does not think that he can go to the meeting and talk about the quality and range of the applications on the system, or which planned enhancements will improve service delivery in what way, as he thinks that both of these topics will be by the by. This meeting is happening at a time of crisis and tough decisions, and his senior managers' expectations of him will be cut accordingly.

He also realizes that if he goes into the meeting and starts to talk about the fear of redundancy that is in the minds of his team members, he will look parochial. He will risk imposing his agenda on the meeting, and might mishandle his opportunity to influence the partners, even though it is an obvious question to discuss, and one he would actually like to talk about. However, he thinks it would be an unwise way to play the meeting, one that might result in his losing influence by putting his own concerns above those that the senior team has in mind to discuss with them. He puts his thinking cap on, determined to use the opportunity he has been given as cleverly as possible.

The technology manager is a loyal man and wants to do the best for his team. He decides that the best way to approach the meeting would be to look at it from the point of view of *his managers' requirements of him*. He asks himself three critical questions:

- What value could I add to the partners' meeting at this time?
- What information, perspective, or facts could I give the partners about the work and outputs of the technology team which would be valuable to their discussions at this meeting?
- What do the partners need to know about the technology team, and me, that demonstrates our worth to the business and proves that it is essential that the firm continue to employ all of us?

He makes careful plans, assembling relevant facts, data, and figures to support his answers, and commits the information to memory. Then he attends the partners' meeting.

The Opportunity to Influence

The technology manager has an opportunity to build on his own excellent reputation with the partners at a time of crisis for the firm. While he is not in a position to decide who will remain in employment and who will be made redundant, he does have a chance to influence the group of people who will make those decisions. He has the chance to use the influence he has already gained with the partners to convince them that, even though this is a tough time for the firm, his technology team is critical to the future success of the business. He needs to convince a weary and stressed group of partners that his team are central to the business, even though they are not fee earners and might therefore be regarded as early candidates for redundancy. He needs to act in ways that are helpful to the partners and supportive of their decision-making processes, so that he can retain influence with them and maximize his opportunity to influence their future decisions.

In order to do this he has to tread a careful line. He needs to add value to the issues the partners want to discuss with him while also selling the merits of his team to the partners *and* reminding them of the benefits of making technology a cornerstone of their plans once the economy picks up again. But, if he fails to use his good reputation wisely at this critical juncture, he may find that the partners' anxiety about losing business causes them to pull back on their half-executed plans to make technology a cornerstone of the business, and the technology team will lose staff. Worse, the technology manager may lose the influence and positive regard he has worked hard for three years to achieve and maintain. If he prioritizes his own fears or his team's fears about their jobs above the issues that the partners want to put to him, he could appear to be out of touch with the tough decisions facing the key decision-making group in the firm, and not up to the job of discussing the hard, unpleasant realities facing the firm. The partners might form the view that he is reliable and useful when things go well, but not so effective or helpful to them when things are harsher.

Handling the Personalities

In order to succeed with his plans to influence the partners the technology manager has to accomplish two things simultaneously. He needs to address the issues that the senior team presents to him, even though he does not know what they will be in advance of the meeting, and he needs to present his own analysis of the value that he and his team add to the firm in an influential and compelling way. He needs to demonstrate to each of the partners that he recognizes the difficult situation the firm is in, and understands that the quality of their decisions at this juncture will have important ramifications for the future of everyone in the firm. He needs to present himself as a proactive, engaged business partner, someone whose specialist technology knowledge results in him having a unique and important perspective on the issues the partners are discussing.

The technology manager decides to listen carefully to the points that the partners put to him before answering them directly and succinctly. Then he determines that, wherever possible, he will make direct links between the issues the partners have raised with him and the answers to the three questions he has prepared. For instance, if the partners ask him for his view on where savings could be made in the technology team, he will suggest a series of realistic alternatives before reminding the partners that:

- The team has added significant value to the firm over the previous three years.
- Technology upgrades have improved client retention until the recent past, and have improved client satisfaction.
- The recent loss of key clients has been down to factors unrelated to the technology team or its performance.
- The plans he has drawn up to improve the technology capability of the firm in the future remain viable and can be restarted once the economy cycles upwards.
- Even though the technology team represents an overhead to the firm, and he recognizes that the firm's costs need to be kept in line with its income during this difficult time, the quality of the technology team and the support it offers the business save the firm money every day, and contribute towards increased client satisfaction.

The technology manager needs to deliver his points in a sober, factual, and respectful way. He cannot afford to let his understandable emotion about potential redundancies in his team affect his demeanor. He needs to be seen to address the business issues in a crisp and serious fashion, so that he matches the mood of the meeting, and sends the partners the message that he understands their dilemma and wants to work with them to resolve the conflicts they face.

The Outcome

The technology manager does a sufficiently good job of influencing the senior team to think carefully before making any technologists redundant that the decisions they take at the end of that meeting include deferring redundancy decisions for one more month. However, the loss of a third major client towards the end of that month makes it inevitable that the firm will lose at least one, and possibly two, people from the technology team.

The technology manager remains in his role, and when the economy cycles upwards towards the end of the year, he is given the go-ahead to proceed with the next tranche of incremental improvements to the system. The partner who informs him of this decision says that his presentation to the partners' meeting at the height of the crisis had the effect of causing them to slow down their speed of decision making over technology redundancies, and, instead take stock. It persuaded them that, while some technology redundancies would be inevitable, they could be deferred, and the firm would aim to retain as many of the technology team as possible.

The technology manager breathes a sigh of relief. He had not known at the time whether or not he had done a good job of influencing the partners about the key role of the technology team in the firm. He had left the meeting worrying that he had not put his case forcefully enough and might have let his team members down. He is relieved to realize that his decision to build influence by positioning his three key sets of points carefully one at a time, while linking them to answers to specific questions put to him by the partners, was a sound and well-executed tactic.

Conclusions

This case study illustrates how to work effectively with the changed priorities of a team of senior managers while also earning the right to influence them to think again before making a series of key decisions. The case study shows that even though the technology manager has a significant agenda of his own – to retain all his staff despite an economic downturn – he needs to adopt a carefully crafted approach to influencing the partners. The stakes are high. If he mishandles the opportunity to influence, he could damage his own reputation with the partners. He could fail to secure the ongoing employment of some members of his team and injure the long-term plans for technology upgrades. To achieve his aims the technology manager needs to adopt an approach that addresses the points put to him by the partners directly and simply, while also introducing carefully selected information calculated to demonstrate the added value he can bring to the partners' meetings, and to demonstrate how valuable the technology team is to the firm. Any other approach runs the risk of appearing out of touch, ill-judged, or irrelevant to the issues with which the partners are grappling, and could result in the technology manager losing the influence he has won, or losing more staff than necessary.

We have just examined an instance of where the factors which brought you influence in the past won't prove effective at helping you retain it in the present, so you need to change tack and utilize different influencing tactics. Let's now turn our attention to a different situation, one in which you recognize that, in order to retain influence, you need to compromise. It's a question of what to compromise over.

KNOWING WHEN TO COMPROMISE

Sometimes you will be in a position where you simply will not be able to get what you want no matter how influential you are, or how well disposed your colleagues usually are to listening to and considering your point of view. It isn't a matter of using the right or wrong influencing tactics, or thinking extra hard about how to position your argument. No matter what tack you take, you will still find that you struggle to bring about the outcomes you want, even though on other issues you have significant influence with the colleagues involved. Why? Simply put, because in that situation, with those issues and those particular colleagues, you will actually harm your reputation if you continue down your chosen influencing route. You need to recognize this fact, step back from the issues, and act in a way that takes into account the bigger picture. You need to make a planned compromise. If you don't, you may waste your energy and time, harm your reputation, and fail to retain some or all of the influence you have previously gained.

The circumstances I am addressing here are those in which you are:

■ Seeking to influence a situation in which some of your colleagues want a different outcome from you, and have just as much political currency and influence as you do. If you continue to push for the outcomes you want, you might either make no headway at all, or worse still, actually galvanize your colleagues into further influencing activity that gains them the upper hand. Rather than risk continuing to invest in a situation in which you cannot succeed, you need to propose a planned compromise and move on.

■ Dealing with a complex issue that has ramifications beyond you and your role. The more you seek to influence the situation, the more likely it will be that additional colleagues learn about your proposals and take an active interest in the issues. They might be better connected than you, and might succeed in getting their plans endorsed instead of yours, so rather than lose big, you decide to settle for an early, planned compromise and place your effort elsewhere.

In both of these situations it is important to assess how likely it will be that you are able to bring about the outcomes you favor, given the level of influence you retain with the decision makers involved in the situation. If you recognize that you are outmatched and losing, pull back and re-evaluate the situation, identifying:

■ Which issues really matter to you.
■ Which factors are less important to you.
■ What compromise would enable you to make some progress even if it isn't the ideal outcome as far as you are concerned.

The benefit of making a planned compromise is that you can secure some of the outcomes you favor while also averting a situation in which you might:

■ Injure effective relationships by continuing to push for outcomes you do not have the influence to secure.
■ Alienate certain colleagues who are well placed and could make trouble for you with influential senior managers.
■ Fail to retain influence with other colleagues with whom you have worked effectively in the past.

However, what happens when you do not have the time to devise a planned compromise? What happens when you make a misjudgment and need to come up with a quick and effective compromise to get yourself out of a tricky situation? Consider the following example, which is set in the Human Resources department of a busy teaching hospital.

The head of HR calls his induction manager into his office and asks him to sit down. The induction manager has a good working relationship with his manager, and considerable influence with his peer group. He is regarded as being hard-working, astute, and capable. The head of HR asks him to take on board a new project, which he then outlines to him. The project involves the induction manager working with his four peers to research the costs and feasibility of outsourcing the in-house staff mentoring service to a private provider.

The induction manager is not at all pleased at being asked to carry such a political hot potato, and shifts uncomfortably in his seat. He decides that his boss is in a difficult position too, and has asked him to lead the project because of his high credibility around the department. Rather than protest, he accepts the challenge, and arranges a meeting with his peers. He uses the meeting to float the idea that the hospital might want to outsource key services to the private sector, and that the five of them are being asked to assess one such option. He observes his colleagues shuffling uncomfortably in their seats. Undeterred, although feeling uncomfortable himself, the induction manager continues to outline the task before them. He tells his colleagues that they are being asked to explore the feasibility of outsourcing the staff mentoring service, and asks for suggested ways forward.

One or two of his colleagues make half-hearted suggestions, before a third colleague points out the invidious position that they have been placed in. He asks the induction manager why he accepted the responsibility of working on this piece of research, and what he hopes to gain by including them in it. The induction manager is embarrassed, and says that as they have been asked to take the project on board by their manager they ought to get on with it. Unfortunately for him, this answer does not satisfy his colleagues, who then ask him to what extent the in-house mentoring team is aware of the possibility they are discussing. The induction manager actually doesn't know, but rather than admit this, he restates his view that they need to get on with the work rather than argue the rights and wrongs of it.

One of his peers pushes back from the table and folds his arms across his chest. Another says that he isn't comfortable discussing the mentoring team behind their backs. The induction manager thinks he is about to lose the active cooperation of the meeting. He suggests that a useful way forward might be for them to brainstorm their reaction to the project they are being asked to carry out, preparatory to outlining a series of steps they would like to see taken next. He facilitates a brainstorm of the various reactions to the project, none of which are positive, then divides the meeting into two groups. Each group has the task of devising a series of next steps to which they are willing to commit personally, all of which will be relayed back in full to the head of HR.

In this situation the induction manager accepts what he knows to be a challenging assignment. He doesn't realize just how difficult it will be to take forward, and perhaps how unwise he was to take it, until he is already in a meeting with his peer group. It is his peers who point out to him the political implications of the project they are being briefed on, and his peers who signal their distaste for the role they are being asked to take in researching the possibility of outsourcing the in-house mentoring department. Sadly for him, the induction manager doesn't respond to the discomfort of his peers in a way which endears him to them. He takes the line that he has been asked by his boss to carry out certain duties, and that he will do so despite the discomfort. His colleagues, however, take a different line. Their view is that the role they have been assigned is unsavory, and it constitutes one they would rather not carry out. They quietly but firmly make their feelings known, and the induction manager quickly realizes that he is about to lose the goodwill of the meeting he is running. He is now faced with a situation in which his peers question him and his judgment, perhaps also question his integrity, and are doing so en masse. He has to find a way forward that:

■ Preserves his reputation with his peer group.
■ Maintains his credibility with his manager.
■ Results in his finding a way forward on the project.

Clearly, this will not be an easy task. He needs to think quickly on his feet, find a compromise that will work, and find it quickly. He presents his suggested way forward in two parts: an opportunity for each person at the meeting to have their say on the project, including what they feel about being asked to take part in it, followed by an opportunity for each of them to outline steps to which they would be personally comfortable committing. He says that all of the proposals will be put to their boss in full. This approach is clever because it:

■ Validates the feelings of his peers.
■ Acknowledges their chagrin at him for putting them in the position they find themselves in.
■ Offers them the opportunity to feed back to their manager on

what they would like to happen next with regards to this particular assignment.

This combination of factors represents an effective compromise for the induction manager. It steers a course between trying to push the issue with colleagues, who might well openly revolt against him should he try to force their hand, and going back to his manager with some constructive suggestions that he might be able to work with rather than nothing useful at all. It is an example of a compromise that works effectively for him, getting him out of a tight situation while creating forward momentum on a politically challenging project.

YOUR INFLUENCING BEHAVIOR

You may now like to identify a situation in which, with the benefit of hindsight, agreeing to a compromise would have proved useful to you. Bring the specific situation to mind and then answer the following questions about it. You can jot down your answers to each of the questions in the space below it:

▪ What was the situation you found yourself in, and whom did you want to influence? In what ways did you want to influence this colleague or colleagues?

▪ What happened when you tried to influence them?

■ Looking back on it now, what compromise could you have sought?

■ What would have been the benefits to you of seeking this compromise?

SUMMARY AND NEXT CHAPTER

This chapter focused on how to retain influence with your colleagues when things are going well for you, and in a variety of adverse situations as well. It:

■ Suggested that one of your key tools for retaining influence is to provide your colleagues with a judicious mixture of a factual analysis of the issue under consideration, coupled with your personal opinion about the way forward given those facts.
■ Highlighted how relying on your opinion when your judgment or conduct is called into question carries reputational risk with it and is best avoided.
■ Proposed that, in these situations, letting the facts speak for themselves is a more astute tactic to use, as it allows your colleagues to come to their own conclusion about you.
■ Suggested that you will need to adjust your approach to influencing senior colleagues as their priorities change, so that your input comes over to them as relevant to the issues *they* are handling.

- Highlighted how offering a compromise solution can be the most advantageous way to handle a politically sensitive issue.
- Included opportunities for you to apply the material to your working life.

The next chapter explores the influencing skills you will need should you find that, while you have an excellent reputation inside your own department, it is not matched by your reputation in the wider organization. The chapter focuses on the influencing skills you will need to promote your profile to more senior and more influential people, people whom you do not work alongside day by day, but who you want to take you seriously when you meet them.

CHAPTER 7

Building a Reputation Outside Your Department

You have high-quality relationships within your team or department. Among those with whom you work day in, day out, you have developed a reputation as someone who works hard, knows their subject matter, and is both confident and competent. Your colleagues see you at work, they observe your committed style, they understand and recognize first-hand the value of the work you do. Your ideas receive sponsorship inside your team or department. People listen to you, consult you, and seek out your opinion. Some may even defer to your point of view. You have influence, and are regarded as an opinion-former on certain issues.

But outside your team or department it's a different story. You struggle to sell yourself to your more senior colleagues in either an impromptu meeting or a scheduled one. When the opportunity arises you don't do a good job of marketing yourself, you have difficulty getting sponsorship for your ideas, and can struggle to get the attention of the more senior and influential people with whom you would like to connect. You realize that you are characterized outside your department as 'lacking impact,' as 'insubstantial,' or as 'not a big player.' Despite your being well regarded in your team or department, outside of it you are seen as someone who is lightweight, lacking influence, gravitas, or clout, and sometimes all three. You are ambitious and work hard, and you want to play a bigger role in the organization. You think you deserve greater responsibility, and believe you could do a more senior role. However, with your current profile that won't happen, and you don't know how to bring about a situation where your reputation becomes a more accurate reflection of your knowledge, application, and endeavor. You are afraid that you will continually be seen as lacking punch, and therefore will unfairly be denied opportunities for advancement.

This chapter is about how to promote yourself outside of your team or department. It shows how to build your profile in the wider organization so that you gain a reputation for being influential, effective, and capable. It demonstrates how to take advantage of the opportunities that come your way to promote yourself, sell yourself, and enhance your reputation outside of your team or department. The chapter will highlight how to behave when you are in the presence of an opinion former or more influential manager, and illustrate how to market your achievements with colleagues whom you don't work alongside day by day. The chapter will focus on the skills of building influence with senior people whom you meet irregularly, and with whom you only have a few minutes or maybe less to make a positive impression.

The chapter will also explore how to alter unhelpful perceptions about you which might have already formed in the minds of some senior colleagues. The chapter enables you to:

- Understand why some colleagues might form the perception that you 'lack substance.'
- Examine a range of behavioral tactics and strategies which will enable you to influence perceptions and challenge unhelpful assumptions which colleagues may have made about you.
- Identify the most effective influencing strategies to use as you seek to handle these situations.
- Be provided with an opportunity to rethink how you position yourself with influential workplace contacts from outside your department or team.

However, the chapter is written with one clear caveat in mind. Its tools and techniques are for those of you who struggle to *present* yourself to your colleagues from other departments. The tools and techniques discussed here are not a substitute for working hard and performing effectively.

IMPROVING YOUR REPUTATION

In my work with clients who want to improve their reputation outside of their team or department, I find that it is often a question of the behavior they use. While the behavior they select makes sense to them and is comfortable for them to use, it is not sufficiently tailored to the specific situation they find themselves in: that of having an opportunity to sell themselves to a more senior and more influential member of the organization who does not work in their department and does not know them or their work very well.

There is usually nothing fundamentally wrong with what they are trying to say. It's more a question of how they are saying it. Very often they need to make adjustments to:

- Where they start their input to the verbal exchange with their colleague.
- The emphasis of what they are saying, so that they make clear what role they play, or have played, in the issues they are describing.
- How they frame their input to make it directly relevant to the agenda of their senior colleague.

Consider the following example.

A talented and hard-working management consultant shares a lift with an influential partner from another division. The consultant is working on a challenging project which he is handling excellently. He has built an influential relationship with his very difficult client, someone who is known for her shortness of temper and her penchant for firing suppliers with whom she quickly becomes impatient. During the short lift ride the partner asks the consultant how the project is going. The consultant is delighted that she knows of his involvement in the project, and emboldened, he tells her that he's been working on it for four weeks now. There are several ways in which the consultant could continue this conversation. Let's examine two of them:

- The consultant knits his brow and says, 'I have had to spend many hours after work taking my client through the process in a series of one-to-one meetings.' He thinks that this statement will demonstrate his personal commitment to his relationship with his client and to the project in general, and he is surprised that the partner doesn't reply to him but instead looks back at him blankly. The partner doesn't speak again, and when the lift reaches her floor she leaves without saying goodbye. She goes back to her desk mentally questioning whether the project is in the right hands or not.
- The consultant looks the partner squarely in the eye and says that the project is going very well and that he is enjoying working on it very much. He then says that every other supplier from every other company that he has encountered during the work finds this client challenging to the point of impossible. 'However,' he continues, 'I have built an excellent relationship with her. She listens to my input and adopts my recommendations. We get on

well.' The partner nods her satisfaction, and when the lift reaches her floor, she gets out without saying goodbye. She returns to her desk and makes a mental note to look for an opportunity to involve this consultant in one of her division's projects in the not too distant future.

MAKING A POSITIVE IMPRESSION

In this situation the consultant has but a few minutes to say the right things in the right way so that he can sell himself to and build his reputation with his more senior colleague. His project is going well and he is confident that he has a good story to tell. Let's revisit the two instances to identify the key differences between the two ways of handling the impromptu meeting.

The First Instance

In the first instance the consultant gets it all wrong. He creates the impression that he is fed up with having to hold his client's hand each evening, when is he actually doing a great job of managing her.

The problem here is threefold. Firstly, the consultant starts his reply to the partner's question in the wrong place. Secondly, he doesn't tell her factually what role he has been playing in the work, how effective he has been at playing it, and what success he has had on the project. Lastly, he doesn't frame his response to make it directly relevant to the partner's real question rather than her stated general question, of 'How is the project going?' Let's take these three critical issues in order, starting with where he begins his reply.

The consultant assumes that the partner knows much more about the project and his involvement in it than she actually does. Instead of giving the partner vital background information about the degree of difficulty posed by this client, and the high-quality relationship he has built with her, he starts mid-story by telling her that he is working late. Understandably she hears this as a complaint, and from this point onwards the wrong impression is being created in her mind. He treats the conversation like an informal chat rather than a selling opportunity, and shoots himself in the foot right from the start.

Secondly, the consultant does not spell out what he has been doing or why he has been doing it. Nor does he describe his success. He does not tell the partner that he is working with a difficult client whom most people find impossible, and has built up a great relationship with her. He doesn't tell her how dedicated and professional a job he is doing for the firm. She doesn't know any of these things, and he doesn't enlighten her. Instead he makes a catastrophic error of presentation. The consultant wants to communicate the effort he has been expending on the project to a senior colleague, in the hopes that the partner will approve of such endeavor and be pleased. He knits his brow and uses the phraseology, 'I have had to …' to describe his investment of time in managing his client. He thinks this form of words will convey his commitment and effort. Instead it creates the impression that he is burdened by the need to spend time with his client, and rather than result in the partner being pleased with him, it results in him securing her disfavor. Actually, he is thoroughly skilled at handling this irascible and unreasonable client, and really enjoying himself, but the partner forms the opposite view because of his poorly chosen words and poor presentation of them.

Lastly, he doesn't address her real question. This isn't a chat in the lift. The partner isn't passing the time of day by asking how it is going. She is asking the question, 'Do I want to work with you?' The consultant doesn't listen properly, doesn't hear the question, and doesn't try to answer it. He misses the opportunity to tell the partner that his client places great faith in him. He misses the opportunity to describe to her the ease with which he has built an influential relationship with this difficult personality. He doesn't tell his senior colleague the fact of the matter: that he is on top of the work and doing a great job in difficult circumstances. Without this information, and because of his apparent complaint about the long hours and the burden of working with this client, the partner forms the view that he isn't doing a good job and isn't trustworthy or capable. So she leaves the lift without speaking again, and with the impression that this consultant might be out of his depth and might need to be replaced.

As a result of this short exchange the partner questions whether someone who is very able isn't actually doing a poor job. She may well give voice to her concerns when speaking with other senior colleagues. She could put doubts into their minds about the consultant, creating mental barriers that he will need to overcome if he finds himself speaking with any of them at some point down the road. The consultant makes the mistake of thinking that 'good work will be rewarded,' so he doesn't try to sell himself to his senior colleague. He now also has a sizeable task ahead of him if he is to reverse the impression he has created, and convince this partner that he is an effective pair of hands.

The Second Instance

In the second instance the consultant does a good job of selling himself. He creates the impression that he is right on top of his project, handling his challenging client excellently, and is energized by the process. He creates this positive impression in a matter of seconds by doing three things well. Let's take a look at each of them in turn.

Firstly, the consultant starts his story at the beginning. He makes no assumptions at all about what the partner might or might not know about his involvement on the project, beyond the fact that he is engaged on it. He simply tells her what he wants her to know in clear, factual terms. He stands tall and looks her confidently in the eye, before telling her that the project is going very well and he is enjoying it. This is a good start, and conveys to the partner that he is confident about what he is doing.

Secondly, he emphasizes the role he is playing in the project, and tells her about the successes he has created. He describes how every other supplier from every other company he has encountered during his work finds this client to be impossible. He states this as a fact, and follows it up with another series of facts: that he has built an excellent relationship with her, she listens to him, she accepts his recommendations, and they get on well. The partner makes up her own mind that this is a skilled consultant, one who understands how critical client management is to the success of a project, and one who can succeed where others have failed.

Thirdly, he frames all his input to this verbal exchange to be relevant to the real agenda of the senior figure. He realizes that this is an important conversation. He realizes that he is being put on the spot and being sussed out. He doesn't fall into the trap of believing that 'good work will automatically be rewarded.' It might be, but he would rather make sure by taking advantage of this opportunity to promote himself. So he gives the partner some key facts, facts that she could easily check out should she want to make sure they are backed up by truth. He gives a factual, fair, and straightforward summary of his involvement on the project, making it more likely that his hard work will be noted, if not actually rewarded at this stage.

As a result of this short exchange the partner forms the view that this consultant is someone with whom she would like to work on one of her division's projects. She nods her head at him and leaves. The consultant has not looked to her for approval. He has not made assumptions about what she does and does not know. Nor has he missed the big opportunity she presents him with when *she* asks *him* about his involvement on the project. He recognizes this key moment for what it is, and sells himself to her. He tells her the fact of the matter. He does not misunderstand what she is actually asking him. He answers her question, and consequently builds his reputation with someone influential and well connected. He will have to perform as effectively in any future ad hoc or scheduled meeting with her, and on any future project in which she involves him. But he has handled this meeting well enough that he will probably be offered the opportunity to do so. And as a result of this short conversation, the partner may well talk about this consultant in favorable terms to other senior colleagues, who will then be predisposed to perceive him in a positive light, whether or not they have worked with him.

This example involves the handy instance of an influential colleague giving a more junior colleague the opportunity to sell himself to her. This is a great opportunity to have, but perhaps not all that common. More often you will have to look for and create opportunities to sell yourself, and sometimes you will need to set out to alter perceptions about you that have already formed in the minds of some of your more influential colleagues. Consider this longer example, which is set in a specialist insurance firm.

CASE STUDY EIGHT: BUILDING A REPUTATION

A quietly ambitious risk assessor is frustrated that his hard work and attention to detail don't come to the notice of the more influential people who run the firm he works in. He is well liked by the colleagues who work alongside him in his own department, and has the full trust and support of his own senior manager. But he doesn't get asked to participate in the more high-profile cross-departmental projects that usually precede rapid advancement in the firm. The risk assessor considers that his omission from these projects is the main reason he is unable to build his profile across the firm. He decides to take steps to address the esteem in which he is held outside of his department. He has a positive relationship with his own senior manager, and talks over his plans with him, gaining his support for his wish to promote his profile outside of the team he works with.

The risk assessor thinks that his approach is slightly counter-cultural in a firm that is renowned for its sober and cerebral style. While most of his colleagues are serious-minded, considered, and unexcitable, he thinks that his strengths include his personable nature, his sense of humor, and his ability to get on with most people. He is an able risk assessor, being both logical and goal-oriented, but he is more sociable and amiable than many of his colleagues, and he worries that these traits work against him.

He decides to arrange a series of meetings with senior managers from outside of his department at which to position his value to the organization. He wants to influence them toward the view that he might be different, but is well worth involving in more high-profile projects. He draws up a list of colleagues to approach, and arranges his first meeting, which is with a senior manager from the corporate team. He selects this senior manager because he is not so elevated that the risk assessor would be unable to get time in his diary, and because this manager is in charge of selecting colleagues to take part in an upcoming cross-departmental project to review the remuneration structure within the firm.

The corporate team manager doesn't really want to meet with the risk assessor, but decides to give him five minutes. His view of him is that he is a bit too lightweight to make it in the firm, but he is open-minded enough to realize that he hasn't worked all that closely with him. The risk assessor starts the meeting by saying that he has had an idea which he thinks might be interesting for the corporate team manager, and wants to run past him. Without pausing for breath he says that he thinks there is an opportunity to cross-sell work from his own department's clients to the clients of the corporate team. He then uses the words: 'I think there is an opportunity for you here to capitalize on existing customer relationships and increase overall revenue.' Then he says that he would like to arrange a meeting between his department's manager and the corporate team's manager. While he says these things he sits upright at the office table and places his forearms and hands on top of it. He leans forward slightly and maintains level eye contact with his more senior colleague.

The corporate team manager considers what he has been told. He is surprised at the quality of the idea, and surprised that it has come from this risk assessor. He agrees to the meeting, and calls his PA straightaway. He asks her to arrange the subsequent meeting for as soon as possible. Then he thanks his colleague for his input, and signals the end of the meeting by standing up. The risk assessor also stands up, and, just before he departs from the table, says in a factual and businesslike tone that he has other ideas he would like to discuss with him at a later date. He leaves a fractional pause before saying that is looking for opportunities to play a role outside his department. He adds that he has his senior manager's approval to do this. Then he smiles, says goodbye, and leaves the room.

The Opportunity to Influence

The risk assessor has a significant opportunity to influence his more senior and influential colleague that he is someone he should seriously consider for, in the first instance, inclusion on a high-profile cross-departmental project. He is an able risk assessor, and if he can build his reputation outside of his department he stands a good chance of advancement. He is aware that part of the problem may lay in his humorous and playful persona. He decides that the best way forward is not to address this issue head on. Instead, he adopts a more considered and serious style while he is in the company of the senior colleague whose opinion of him he wishes to influence, and decides to give him a good idea, one that will be of benefit to him, and which will hopefully cause the senior man to reappraise him. Outside of these meetings, and back in his own department where is credibility is not in doubt, he can relax and adopt his usual relational style. But when he is engaged in a meeting to build his profile he determines to use a more cerebral and businesslike approach in order to avoid the situation where his colleagues make value judgments about him simply because he is different.

Handling the Personalities

In order to succeed in his plans to present himself as worthy of inclusion in the upcoming cross-departmental project, the risk assessor needs to present both his idea and himself in the most advantageous light to the corporate team's manager. The risk assessor needs to come off as sober, and he needs to present his idea as a valuable service to his more influential colleague. He handles himself well.

His selection of this colleague is a good start. The corporate team manager is influential but not out of the risk assessor's league, and he is about to set up the important intra-firm project. He is well positioned to influence whether or not the risk assessor will be included on the project. However, he is also an impatient man, and doesn't really rate the risk assessor that highly. Although he doesn't know it, the risk assessor actually only has five minutes in which to make his mark with him, and he uses his time well. He:

- Adopts a focused, crisp approach from the start of the meeting.
- Gets down to business straight away.
- Sits forward, denoting his interest in the conversation and his engagement with the issues he wants to speak about.
- Sets the scene by saying that he has something to say which he thinks might be of interest to the corporate team manager.
- Presents his idea factually, and then personalizes it to make it clear that it is an idea that he thinks is valuable specifically to the corporate team manager. He does this with the words, 'I think there is an opportunity for you here to capitalize on existing customer relationships and increase revenue.'
- Then he suggests a way forward: a meeting between his departmental senior manager and the corporate team manager.

At this point everything has gone according to plan. He has made his points succinctly, factually, and soberly, and has presented them as a service to his more influential colleague. He has gained the interest of his colleague sufficiently that the corporate team manager asks his PA to arrange the subsequent meeting then and there. At this point, however, his senior colleague doesn't do what the risk assessor would like. He doesn't offer him anything in return. In fact when he asks his PA to set up the subsequent meeting, he doesn't even suggest that the risk assessor be involved. The corporate team manager may simply assume that the risk assessor will be present, but the risk assessor cannot be sure about this. He isn't thrown, and adopting the same sober and determined style, he says that he has other ideas which might be of interest to him. After a minute's pause he drops the idea into the manager's mind that he is looking for an opportunity to play a role beyond his department, and that his own boss is OK with this.

The risk assessor cleverly handles this potentially tricky moment. He avoids:

- Embarrassing the corporate team manager or himself by asking directly to be included in the next meeting.
- Undoing all his good work by appearing to be put out at not being offered something in return for his good idea.

Instead he makes it clear that he has more to offer, is ambitious, and is well thought of by his own boss. The corporate team manager is astute enough not to offer the risk assessor a place on his forthcoming project then and there, but he has heard the offer of a bargain. He may well decide that it would be worth his while to offer the risk assessor a place at that particular table, both for the value he could add to the project, and for the options it will give him to pick his brains further regarding his other good ideas.

The final point for the risk assessor to consider is how to handle the upcoming meeting between his senior manager and the corporate team manager. Perhaps the best way forward for him would be to suggest to his boss that he be included. He will need to adopt the same serious, dignified persona at the second meeting if he is to continue to create the kind of impression he wants with the corporate team manager, and influence him that his hard work and creative ideas merit attention.

The Outcome

The risk assessor creates an opening for himself in the wider firm. His selection of which colleague to approach and over what, coupled with his judicious and well-crafted handling of the meeting, create a situation in which he secures for himself a place on the forthcoming project team, along with the opportunity it provides to meet other influential colleagues from the wider firm. However, he needs to be assiduous in seeking out and taking advantage of further opportunities to add value to the firm outside his own department if he is to secure the level of influence he would like to have. He cannot assume that inclusion on one intra-firm project will be enough to alter perceptions wholesale. It is a good start, but he has much more work to do yet.

Conclusions

The risk assessor takes responsibility for managing his reputation. He realizes that a combination of his sociable persona, as well as his comparatively low-key profile in the wider firm, have resulted in a situation where he is not that well regarded outside of his own department. He avoids the pitfall of thinking that his supportive boss is responsible for finding him the kind of opportunities he wants, and sets out to look for them himself. He decides to slowly and steadily build his profile and reputation outside of his department. Only time will tell how effective he will be at doing this, but the initial signs are that he has the judgment and skill to do a good job.

YOUR INFLUENCING BEHAVIOR

We have been examining a situation in which an ambitious colleague seeks to enhance his reputation outside of his own department. You may now like to apply this material to your own working life. Consider the following questions. You can jot down your answers to each of the questions in the space below it:

- With which senior colleague from outside of your department would you like to build influence?

- What is your specific aim in building your profile with this colleague?

- What opportunities exist for you to start to do this?

- What influencing strategy will you use? What will be your first and subsequent steps?

So far we have been considering situations where reputations are improved or injured in the course of a few minutes. What about a situation where a colleague needs to alter the unfair perception that she is performing below par, a perception that is widely held and which has developed over time? Consider the following case study, which is set in an engineering firm.

CASE STUDY NINE: ALTERING PERCEPTIONS

An able quality control engineer with an understated style is headhunted to join an engineering firm which produces electrical components. She joins the firm as the head of quality, and quickly settles in. She enjoys her job, and likes her team members, with whom she enjoys a degree of rapport. But, after a few months, she begins to feel increasingly frustrated with her peer group, whom she thinks of as too keen to rush to a decision without having given sufficient thought to alternative options.

She begins to see herself as a bit different from her peers, characterizing them, not unkindly, as more opinionated, energetic, and tough-minded than she is. She does not doubt their competence as engineers or as managers, but forms the view that her quietly determined and more practical style is uncomfortable for some of her more direct colleagues. This view is given further weight when her six-monthly appraisal includes comments about her realistic and reserved approach, comments that come over to her as slightly denigrating. These comments are included in the 360-degree feedback section of her appraisal, and although they are not attributed to members of her peer group, she decides that that is from where they originate.

Following her appraisal she begins to notice a difference in her boss's attitude to her. She thinks he becomes more skeptical and less open to her. She thinks he is a bit less receptive to her points of view. None of these reactions is so marked or obvious that she could pick him up on them, but over a period of weeks, they coalesce in her mind into the view that he does not rate her as highly as he did when he recruited her to join the firm. She doesn't know what to put this altered perception down to. She meets all her key performance indicators and continues to work well with her team. But the doubt remains in her mind that her peers don't like certain things about her low-key style, and she thinks that their view might have communicated itself to her boss.

Nonetheless, she is surprised when, a few weeks later, her boss calls her into his office and tells her that he would like to talk to her about one or two issues with her style. He explains that he would like her to work with a coach to help her make a more positive impression with her peers and seniors. He stresses that he knows she works hard, achieves her key performance indicators, and is well regarded by her team. But he tells her that her style poses certain issues with her peer group, who regard her as a bit detached and theoretical. The head of quality pauses while she considers her response. She says that her performance is measured by her ability to achieve her key performance indicators, something that she has unfailingly done since joining the firm. She tells her boss that she is skeptical about the feedback and would like to understand what it means.

Her boss explains to her that she comes across as being insufficiently authoritative and credible. He says that he doesn't doubt her engineering ability or the rigor of her approach. It's more that she doesn't put herself across in a way that does her justice. He says he would like her to adopt a more convincing and imposing style. He says somewhat condescendingly that in the firm, having the technical ability is only the start. True authority and influence come from the way in which a senior colleague interacts with their peers and senior managers.

The head of quality is stung. She feels patronized. She considers that the feedback she has just been given reflects a series of value judgments about her made by her peer group and her boss. She tells her boss that she considers that the feedback is more a reflection of subjective reactions to the difference she brings to the firm than it is an objective comment about her performance or her value to the company. Nonetheless, she accepts that the perception she creates does matter, and decides that she will work with a coach to address these issues and make a series of behavioral adjustments to counteract the value judgments being made about her.

Over the next month she works with a coach, and steps back from her relationships with her peer group. The coach helps her to begin to see herself through the eyes of people who use a different style, do things for a different reason, and adopt different behavior from her. With the help of the coach she starts to behave differently when she is with her peers and senior managers. Specifically, she realizes that, even though she doesn't see it this way herself, her low-key style could appear to lack influence to other people. She thinks that she might take too long to make her points. She thinks that she might need to think things through for a bit longer or in more detail than her colleagues, and that she might appear to be too reliant on other people's points of view. She thinks that cumulatively the behaviors she uses might create the impression that she lacks confidence when actually she is quite sure of herself.

She works with her coach on a weekly basis. Over a period of a few weeks she decides to make a series of specific changes to her behavior in the hope of altering the perceptions of her peers and her manager. During this process she keeps her boss updated about the outcomes from the coaching meetings. Then she arranges to meet the peer whom she considers to be her main detractor. She goes to his office for the meeting and sits across the desk from him. She tells him that she has been engaged in a development process that has opened her eyes to one or two things. She tells him that she has learned to do some things differently over the past few weeks. She tells him that she would like to think that he and she would be able to work together going forward. There is an edge of challenge about this comment. Her tone is factual and harder than her more usual style. She makes and keeps firm eye contact with him throughout the meeting, and when she is ready to end the meeting she does so with the minimum of fuss. She simply gets up and leaves the room, closing the door behind her.

The Opportunity to Influence

In this case study the head of quality has the opportunity to correct an unfair perception that her performance is below par. The perception is rooted in the fact that her style is counter-cultural to the style that predominates among her peer group. Her peers make a series of value judgments about her, judgments that are largely subjective, and which come to influence the perception that her own manager holds about her as well.

However, she is clear-headed enough to realize that while this situation may be unfair, it isn't going to go away. Her ability to achieve her key performance indicators is not in doubt, but she knows she cannot do her job without the active support of her peers and her boss. She recognizes that she needs to turn their perceptions around so that they come to see her as someone who is active, capable, and confident. She realizes that, no matter how effective her relationships are with her team members, she cannot afford to behave in ways that result in her peers and manager asking questions about her. She decides that the best way forward is to work on adopting behavior that this group of people regards as influential and credible.

Fortunately for her she has a boss who is willing to invest in her. He provides her with a budget with which to work with a coach to help her find suitable behavioral adjustments. She needs to find the right balance between playing to her own strengths and behaving in ways that get the attention of her peer group. If she can get this balance right, she stands a good chance of:

- Getting her peers off her back.
- Reducing the amount of unwelcome feedback she has to deal with.
- Encouraging her peers to give more weight to her opinions.
- Playing a full and influential role in peer meetings.
- Altering an unduly harsh assessment of her based on value judgments about her.
- Arresting the slide in her boss's perception of her.

If she cannot bring about these changes she may well continue to lose the respect of her peers, and possibly lose her boss's goodwill too. Under these circumstances she will find it increasingly difficult to carry out her work, and no matter how effective she is at meeting her key performance indicators, may find her role becomes a difficult one.

Handling the Personalities

The head of quality has some work to do if she is to turn around the prejudicial perceptions that her peer group hold about her. She needs to get some objective input so that she can make the right behavioral changes in the right way. She realizes that she will have to adopt, on a consistent basis, behavior that her peer group regard as influential. She may or may not agree with their definition of what does or does not constitute influential behavior. In fact she is likely to regard their definition as narrow, restricted only to behaviors that they use themselves or behaviors that are close to those they use themselves. Nonetheless, she has joined a peer culture in which certain behaviors are regarded as influential, and in which certain behaviors are not. If she is to stay in her role and be effective at a senior level, she will need to adopt behavior that is consistently regarded as persuasive by her peers and manager.

She works diligently at identifying these behaviors with her coach, and equally hard at applying them in situations in which she meets her peers. She wisely keeps her manager updated about the outcomes from the coaching meetings. She does this to ensure that he realizes how seriously she is taking the process, and to apprise him of the return he can expect on his investment in her. After a few weeks of identifying and employing selected new behavior she feels confident enough to take the next step.

She arranges a meeting with the peer whom she regards as the most serious of her critics. She wants to put a marker down with this peer, a marker that tells him she is there to stay and he will have to deal with her. Her approach to this meeting is understated with a hard edge of resolve. She tells him that she has learned one or two things recently without saying what she is referring to. This puts a question into his mind about what point she is addressing. Her hardened tone alerts him to the fact that she is in a different mode to those he has encountered before. He hears the challenge. Then she goes onto the front foot and tells him that she 'would like to think that you and I could work together going forward.' This is a calculated risk on her part, one calculated to tell him that she is watching him just as much as he is watching her, and that as far as she is concerned, she is now up to speed. Having placed her cards on the table she simply leaves the room quietly and without further ado.

Only time will tell how this peer hears this contretemps and what interpretation he places upon it. But he can be in no doubt that she is a different animal, and less lacking in what he might see as personal power or self-regard than he thought she was at the time of her six-monthly evaluation.

The Outcome

Working with a coach gives the head of quality the input and objective feedback she needs to enable her to make the right behavioral changes as quickly as possible. Keeping her boss updated keeps her on the right side of him as she makes these changes. Confronting her peer wins her the respect she needs from him, and along with her new suite of behaviors, it causes him to reappraise her and begin to take her more seriously. Over a period of time she gains back the ground she had lost to her peers, and while her relationships with them will never be easy or relaxed, she learns how to behave when she is around them so that she can prevent them dismissing her ideas and proposals on purely stylistic interpretations. She becomes more influential in peer meetings, and continues to enjoy a positive relationship with her boss. However, she is also aware that if she slips back into her more innate, low-key behavior, even for just one meeting, she will undo a lot of the good work she had done up to that point. She is well aware that she needs to use her suite of new behaviors each and every time she meets with one of her peer group.

Conclusions

The lessons from this case study are that perceptions matter, and poor perceptions can be turned around. The head of quality does not think that the perceptions her peers hold about her are fair, but she realizes that if she wants to continue to operate at a senior level in this firm, she has to deal with them. She does the wise thing in seeking to alter her peers' perceptions by making behavioral changes rather than engaging with them in a debate about the relative merits of her style as opposed to theirs. She is prepared to use new behavior and assess to what extent it contributes to a fresh perception in her peers' minds. Fortunately for her, while her peers prove themselves capable of making value judgments against her, they subsequently prove themselves capable of making value judgments in her favor too. Her political stock rises and her influences increase. She spends less time having to assimilate feedback she doesn't agree with, and more time doing the job she enjoys.

YOUR INFLUENCING BEHAVIOR

We have been examining a situation in which a series of colleagues form an unfairly biased view of a peer simply because of their own value judgments about her. You may now like to apply this material to your own working life. Consider the following questions. You can jot down your answers to each of the questions in the space below it:

■ Identify a colleague from outside your department or team who you think doesn't regard you as being as credible as you would like. Who is this colleague? What leads you to think they don't rate you that highly?

■ What value judgments do you think they have made about you?

■ In what ways would you like to alter their perception?

■ How will you bring about this change in their perception? What will be your first and subsequent steps?

SUMMARY AND NEXT CHAPTER

This chapter has focused on how to build influence with colleagues who don't work alongside you day by day, and who don't regard your natural way of doing things as influential. It:

■ Explored how even short exchanges with more influential colleagues can have a significant impact on your reputation in their eyes, and on the way in which they subsequently speak about you to their peers.
■ Highlighted how giving a full, factual account of your involvement in a project along with a summary of the successes you have

had on it is essential if you are to take advantage of opportunities to sell yourself to senior colleagues.

- Suggested that you need to develop a specific suite of influencing behaviors if you want to raise your profile outside of your department or team.
- Proposed that you might need to put together a plan to enable you to systematically build influence with key colleagues.
- Examined how building and retaining influence is as much about the behavior you use as your technical effectiveness in your role.
- Identified how important it is to adopt behavior that is regarded as influential in the culture in which you work, even if it isn't natural for you, if you are to avoid value judgments being made about you by your more culturally attuned colleagues.
- Included opportunities for you to apply the material to your working life.

The next chapter explores the influencing skills you will need should you find yourself working with irresponsible and work-shy colleagues, who are comfortable letting others do the work while they manipulate senior colleagues' perceptions.

CHAPTER 8

Influencing Irresponsible Colleagues

It's straightforward to work with responsible colleagues: people who want to work hard, get things done, make the right things happen at the right time, and who work productively toward their goals in tandem with you and with their other colleagues. These co-workers may from time to time lack the diary space or the inclination to consult with you as fully as you would like, or to be available to you when you seek their input, and they may not always listen to your views or involve you in their decision-making and problem-solving processes when you want them to. But they are otherwise uncomplicated co-workers to have, people who understand the value of hard work, want to build effective workplace relationships, and enjoy the rewards that rightly come to them for their responsible and committed approach. Many of your colleagues are likely to handle their working lives and responsibilities along these lines.

However, it gets more confusing and more troublesome when you are asked to work with a different kind of colleague, someone who doesn't always want to work hard, isn't always industrious, and who may well look for opportunities to coast. These colleagues prefer to come to work and get by, doing just enough and muddling through. Some of these co-workers are skilled at appearing to be busy when they are actually not doing very much at all. Others simply approach their work in a slipshod and careless way, and don't care that their outputs are often below par. Fortunately, you probably don't have to handle this kind of irresponsible conduct all that frequently but, when you do, it is wearisome to deal with.

Many of these irresponsible colleagues do have a key skill. They have learned how to manipulate their senior colleagues' perceptions. Some of them are accomplished at acquiring the credit for other people's work. They present themselves effectively to decision makers, opinion formers, and influential managers, and are often regarded as effective and capable employees by those who manage them. Some of them are skilled at sloping shoulders whenever something goes wrong, and are quick to ensure that any accountability that really should sit with them or their team skips past them and lands on someone else instead.

The problem for you, should you find yourself working with colleagues like these, is that you may well end up doing most or all of the work yourself, including worrying about the fact that your colleague isn't contributing very much to the process. The challenge for you is to find effective ways of building influence with your irresponsible colleague. Your usual influencing toolkit simply won't do it. This challenge requires a specific suite of influencing skills, and it is these skills that are the subject of this chapter.

This chapter will focus on the art of influencing an irresponsible colleague. It will highlight how to influence a negligent co-worker toward adopting a more productive approach to your joint work, while safeguarding your own reputation as someone who wants to perform effectively. The chapter will help you to:

- Understand why some colleagues adopt a work-shy or manipulative approach at work.
- Identify the most effective influencing strategies to use as you seek to handle these features of their conduct.
- Highlight the pitfalls of using an ineffective or flawed approach to influencing irresponsible colleagues.
- Apply the material to your own working life.

THE PROFILE OF AN IRRESPONSIBLE COLLEAGUE

Most of you are likely to go to work and be fully focused on doing a good job. You apply yourselves to the projects and tasks you are paid to manage. You want to complete them in the best possible way and to the highest possible standards. You set out to handle your relationships with your colleagues in an above-board and straightforward way. From time to time you may make mistakes and mess up. You may get your priorities wrong and give insufficient attention to important tasks. You may let your standards slip, or you may misread situations which you consequently handle less well than you could have. But none of these situations arises because you consciously intend to be evasive, lazy, or casual about your work. They are more likely to be the result of genuine mistakes, tiredness, overwork, or simple errors of judgment on your part.

Contrast that way of doing things with the approach of colleagues who are deliberately conniving and lethargic, who don't want to work hard, and who have trouble with both commitment and responsibility. These colleagues want to get by while appearing to be busy. They prefer to keep close to the influential people in the organization. They want to acquire influence and kudos, but seek to achieve these aims without producing very much or actually doing very much. Some of these colleagues consistently produce substandard work and hope to get away with it, while others become skilled at manipulating the perceptions of key opinion formers and decision makers. They make sure that, while many of their more conscientious colleagues are engaged in moving projects forward, their more influential colleagues form the view that they are the ones who are really directing things and without whom the projects would fail. They are skilled at managing their images and acquiring political currency.

In order to avoid responsibility for producing sloppy work, and in order to keep up the illusion that they are vital and productive members of the workforce, these colleagues have acquired a well-developed suite of interpersonal tools. When put on the spot by co-workers frustrated at their slack or calculating approach, they become adept at:

- Dodging the questions put to them.
- Creating fog around the issues they are asked to address.
- Obfuscating and changing the emphasis of the conversation away from the issue of their conduct.
- Placing responsibility back with the colleague calling them to account.
- Disowning their behavior if cornered.

These behaviors can be infuriating to encounter and very difficult to deal with. They can leave you feeling angry, powerless, and confused, or all three. In this mode an irresponsible colleague can be very hard to influence. You can call a meeting to confront your colleague, and leave it feeling that somehow you became the subject of the debate rather than them. You can form the view that the meeting achieved nothing of any value, and indeed, that your relationship with the irresponsible colleague has become more difficult, not less so.

However, even more irritating can be the realization that senior managers believe that your irresponsible colleague is central to progress on a project, when it is you and your co-workers who are actually doing the work. To pressured and time-conscious senior managers, irresponsible colleagues can become adept at presenting themselves as reliable, active, and engaged. However, to those of you who are actually doing the work and who have to work with their uncooperative and obstructive behavior, these conclusions can give rise to dismay and create a degree of cynicism.

EXAMPLES OF IRRESPONSIBLE BEHAVIOR

Consider the following short examples:

- An irresponsible and sloppy banker fails to provide his quality-conscious peer with the information she needs to complete her own work on time. The more conscientious colleague confronts her co-worker about his failure to meet the agreed deadline for delivering the information. She points out to him that he did not contact her before the deadline to warn her that he was going to miss it. Nor has he contacted her since the deadline to account for why he missed it and deliver the information. Her arguments about quality, service standards, and basic courtesy are met with a lack of interest, and she leaves the meeting without the information she needs.

- An irresponsible research scientist receives an email from his more diligent accounts colleague pointing out that his recent questions about expense codes and costs have gone unanswered. The research scientist simply deletes the email and then ignores two subsequent follow-up messages which he retrieves from his telephone voice message system. When the exasperated accountant comes to his office to ask for the information face to face, he makes the mistake of assuming that the research scientist has good reasons for failing to answer his queries. He begins the meeting by empathizing with his colleague's heavy workload, and suggests to him that his lack of understanding of the accounts process might be the problem. He offers to take him through it again. The irresponsible colleague laughs at him, and picks up the phone to make a call, leaving him sitting there bewildered.

- A drug company saleswoman is confronted by her more assiduous peer who tells her that her client update reports are inaccurate, inconsistent, and poorly presented. She states that this state of affairs reflects badly on the sales team as a whole. Her more dedicated colleague complains vehemently to her that she cannot sanction letting such a poor piece of work out of the department, and tells her co-worker that she stayed until 10 pm the previous night reworking the document. The irresponsible colleague is simply amused by how hot under the collar her peer is getting about the issue, and offers platitudinous responses to her requests for more accurate and timely reporting in future. But her subsequent reports continue to be presented in as imprecise and inexact terms as the one that occasioned the complaint, and her colleague continues to intercept them and work late to amend them.

In each of these examples workplace relationships are strained by the actions of one colleague who thinks that their irresponsible conduct is acceptable. In each case the irresponsible colleague is confronted over their behavior, but in none of the cases do they feel the need to amend their approach. In each instance the colleague who did the confronting used arguments that made complete sense to them, but that proved ineffective and failed to yield the results they expected. Even though they couldn't have known it at the start of their influencing conversation, in each case the more industrious colleague mishandled the opportunity to build influence. Let's examine some of the issues.

MISHANDLING IRRESPONSIBLE COLLEAGUES

In each of these cases the more responsible colleague fails to influence their irresponsible colleague toward adopting a more dependable, high-quality approach. As a consequence they:

- Invest time and effort in organizing and contributing to a futile meeting.
- Don't get the information they need and so can't complete their own tasks on time.
- Suffer the indignity of being ridiculed or having their concerns reduced to unimportant.
- Work late to cover for their irresponsible colleague out of a misplaced sense of duty to their employer.

However, it isn't only that. After the meeting the more responsible colleague still has to work alongside the irresponsible one. It is still beholden upon them to find ways of handling their colleague's negligent behavior effectively so that they don't find themselves in the same situation again. What can they do to make sure that they build sufficient influence with their colleague that they don't end up doing the work that their irresponsible colleague should be doing, or worse, find themselves unable to carry out their own work because of the obstructive tactics of their co-worker?

Let's explore the options by considering the following longer example, which is set in the facilities management department of an accountancy firm.

CASE STUDY TEN: HELD TO ACCOUNT

A busy facilities management team in a large accountancy firm is fully engaged with a series of office moves following the completion of an extension to the firm's main office building. A number of these moves prove to be complicated and difficult to accomplish. Towards the end of the planning phase on a particularly difficult move, the head of department decides to reward her team for their hard work and takes them out for a meal after work. During her short after-dinner speech she singles out one member of staff for particular praise for her work on the tax department move. In front of the entire team she says that this member of staff's hard work and skill at handling a difficult political situation has been noted by the head of tax.

Late on the following day the head of the facilities management department receives a telephone call from the head of tax. He says that he has received an email from a member of the facilities management team which has surprised him. The email casts doubt on the professionalism of the staff member who the head of department publicly praised the previous evening. Worse still, it claims credit for her work. The email comes from another member of the facilities management team, one whom the head of facilities management regards as a sloppy and careless member of the department. The head of facilities management asks her internal client to forward the email to her immediately, and on putting down the receiver, she calls the team member who allegedly wrote it into her office.

There are several ways in which the head of facilities management could handle this meeting. Let's explore three of them:

■ She asks her team member to come in and sit down before telling him that she has just had a call from the head of tax. She demands angrily that he explain himself. Her team member remains calm and relaxed and stays sitting in his chair despite the fact that his boss is standing up. He tells her that he doesn't know what she is talking about. The head of facilities management is completely thrown, and in the time it takes her to find her words, her team member tells her that he has to get back to work because he has a lot on. He stands up and leaves the room.

■ She asks her team member to come in and invites him to sit down. Then she tells him that she has had some feedback about him which has concerned her and says she wants to talk it through with him. She tells him that she has just been speaking with the head of tax who has received his email. She pauses for effect before saying that she will not condone one member of her team bad-mouthing another and taking credit for her work. Her team member merely looks at her blankly before asking her the blunt question, 'Is that it?'

■ She meets her team member at the door and asks him to come in. She offers him a seat before returning to her desk and opening her email inbox. She takes the time to print out the email which the head of tax has forwarded to her since their call ended. She collects the email from the printer and returns to her seat across from her team member. She makes level eye contact with him, and using a steady and paced manner of delivery, says, 'You have written an email undermining a colleague's professionalism and taking credit for her work, and you have sent it to a client.' Then she lets a silence fall while she maintains steady eye contact with him. Her team member breaks eye contact with her for a moment and then re-establishes it, but he doesn't speak. She waits for him to settle again, and says in as composed as voice as she can manage, 'I will be meeting the head of tax later this week, and I want you to attend the meeting.' The team member stiffens and she watches the color drain from his face.

The Opportunity to Influence

The head of facilities management has the opportunity to influence her team member toward amending his behavior. Specifically, she wants to influence him to:

■ Cease being careless and shoddy in his approach to his own work.
■ Commence applying himself more stringently to his duties.

- Achieve a consistently higher standard of work.
- Cease trying to take the credit for work he hasn't done.
- Cease trying to undermine his teammates behind their backs.
- Cease contacting a colleague's clients without either their or her say-so.
- Take responsibility for his duplicitous behavior.
- Apologize to his co-worker.
- Make amends with the head of tax.

If the head of facilities management fails to influence her team member to take a more responsible line and amend his errant ways, she will have a battle with him from that moment onwards. He will gain the upper hand, and she will find that it becomes harder to influence him in the future. He will learn that, should he wish to take credit for someone else's work in future, he will probably get away with it then too.

Handling the Personalities

Let's explore the three instances to examine how the head of facilities management handles her irresponsible team member.

The First Instance

In the first instance the head of facilities management uses her anger to confront her team member. Unfortunately for her this strategy doesn't work at all. In fact, it hands him the initiative. She does feel genuinely angry with him, both for his attempt to undermine a hard-working colleague and for his attempt to take credit for her work. She is also appalled that he should do so in such a duplicitous and downright sneaky way. She lets her feelings be known, but sadly for her, plays right into his hands. She assumes that, when confronted, he will simply come clean, hold his hands up, and admit to wrongdoing. When he doesn't she is completely thrown. In the silence that follows her angry words, he seizes the initiative. He tells her that he doesn't know what she is talking about, and while she stands there stunned and amazed, he leaves the room. Why did her anger not influence him to own up and take responsibility?

Mainly because he doesn't regard his behavior as reprehensible, even though any other member of her team might do so. This team member isn't responsible, doesn't think about the consequences of his actions for himself or for anyone else, and doesn't consider that his conduct in sending the email to the head of tax was ill-advised or culpable. He is, to some extent, without concern about it. When his boss is angry with him he simply shrugs it off. He doesn't care that she is cross. He doesn't care that he has hurt a co-worker. He simply takes control of the meeting, turns his boss's anger back on her, and says that he is busy. He reduces her righteous anger to irrelevant triviality, and leaves the room with his boss open-mouthed and defeated. She has used an ineffective approach, and will now have to work twice as hard to regain the ground she has just lost.

The Second Instance

In the second instance the head of facilities management uses a less angry and more assertive approach. She tells her team member that she has had some feedback about him which has concerned her. She pauses for emphasis, and then says that she cannot condone one team member taking the credit for another team member's work. She fully expects this statement to have a devastating effect on a guilty team member. But it doesn't, and she is amazed to find that he simply stares back at her and says, 'Is that it?' He seems completely unaffected by her words or her authority in saying them. She is his boss, and yet he has displayed contempt for her reprimand, and turned the tables on her, all in one short, three-word response. In fact, he seems to be calling her to account, having made her judgment and reading of the situation the problem, rather than his behavior in originating the issue. How can he appear so nonchalant?

He appears so nonchalant mainly because he is unconcerned about being reprimanded in this manner. It doesn't really bother him that his boss has 'told him off.' He isn't upset, embarrassed, or annoyed. He regards his boss's words as a slap on the wrist at best, and an opportunity to put the ball back into her court. Once more she has unwittingly used an ineffective approach. With any other member of her team this reprimand would prove persuasive. But with this irresponsible team member it doesn't, and she loses ground.

The Third Instance

In the third instance the head of facilities management handles her team member well, and although she wouldn't know it from how he behaves at the time, she has gone some way to influencing him not to repeat his trick in future. What does she do that proves so influential?

Firstly, she takes control of the room and the meeting straight away. She meets him at the door and allows him to come into the room. This signals to him that he is entering her space. She then offers him a seat and ignores him while she selects the head of tax's email from her inbox and prints it out. This relegates the irresponsible team member to an observer while retaining her control of the proceedings. When she is ready she returns to her seat and addresses him.

Secondly, when she speaks she doesn't display any visible emotion. She isn't obviously angry, upset or scathing. She uses a steady, measured pace of delivery, which denotes that she means every word she is saying, and that he had better listen. Her facial expression remains outwardly calm and collected, so that he cannot use her emotion against her by telling her that her perception is at fault rather than his conduct.

Thirdly, when she confronts him she presents him with the fact of the matter. She tells him that he has sent an email, that he has sent it to an internal client, that it undermines a colleague, and that in it he takes credit for her work. These are facts, and she presents them as facts. She doesn't say, 'I know what you have been doing,' which would make the conversation about what she does or does not know, and which would present him with another opportunity to deny or obfuscate. Instead she presents his actions as facts, and lets the facts speak for themselves. She tells him that he has written an email undermining a colleague's professionalism, has taken credit for her work, and has sent it to a client. He is cornered, and breaks eye contact with her, his only visible sign of discomfort at that point. She drives home her advantage by telling him that she wants him to attend a meeting with the head of tax which she is arranging. This is her coup de grace. She doesn't say why she wants him to attend the meeting, but he can have a good idea that it won't be comfortable for him. She might require that he apologize, or she might give him another dressing down in front of the head of tax. Either way the team member knows that it will be an uncomfortable meeting for him, and that he won't be able to wriggle out of it easily. He may be thick skinned but he isn't made of steel, and his reputation will take a public hit as a result of this meeting.

How might he respond? He could suggest that she is mistaken, in which case all the head of facilities management has to do is to hand him the email she has printed out. He could say that someone other than him has sent the email from his computer, in which case his boss could say, 'I don't quite believe you.' This makes a distinction between what he says and the truth, which she reserves the right to determine for herself. He will be completely stymied.

As it is he doesn't say anything, and she watches the color drain from his face. While he won't say so, she can be reasonably assured that he is unlikely to try that particular tactic again. She will have to follow through and arrange the meeting with the head of tax, to prove to her errant team member that she means what she says, and she will have to ask him to either apologize or set the record straight. But her tactic of making sure that he feels discomfort as a result of his duplicitous actions is highly likely to be influential, and will probably influence him not to repeat them again.

The Outcome

In the first instance the facilities manager unwittingly shoots herself in the foot when she finds that her indignation at her team member's behavior doesn't influence him at all. In fact she finds that he uses her anger against her. He walks out of her office leaving her feeling foolish and powerless. In the second instance the facilities manager also fails to influence her colleague. She finds that her confrontation with her team member only results in his playing down the situation to such a point that he deflates her. Only in the third instance, one in which the facilities manager creates discomfort for her team member, does she hold sway. Her response to his irresponsible and duplicitous behavior is to make sure that he feels the pain his actions deserve. Only then will he be motivated to alter his behavior.

Conclusions

Only when the facilities manager uses specific influencing tools designed for dealing with an irresponsible member of her workforce will she find a way of handling this situation to her satisfaction. These tools are to:

- Take control of the meeting at the start through her behavior rather than her words.
- Use a calm and steady tone, one that is not angry or passionate, but that is measured and clear throughout the interview.
- Outline her team member's actions as a series of facts that cannot be disputed.
- Make it clear that, as a direct result of his irresponsible actions,

there will be unpleasant consequences for the team member to deal with, consequences that it will be awkward and embarrassing for him to handle.

This last point is vital. It is the expectation and subsequent reality of personal discomfort – of personal embarrassment – that influences the irresponsible team member toward ceasing his duplicitous and underhand activity. His boss's anger alone won't do it. The expectation, and subsequent reality, of his personal discomfort will.

CONFRONTING IRRESPONSIBLE BEHAVIOR

Many irresponsible colleagues get away with their negligent approach either because their colleagues mishandle their confrontations with them, or because someone else more diligent, but actually quite unwise, bails them out. This second colleague covers for them, picks up their work for them, excuses them, or unknowingly misinterprets their willful irresponsibility as justifiable, perhaps thinking it the result of not understanding a process well enough or of being overworked. As a result of this approach the irresponsible colleague is enabled in their irresponsibility and has no reason to change their approach. It is only when colleagues stop covering for the irresponsible co-worker and let them feel the unpleasant consequences of their actions that will they be influenced to change tack.

However, as we have just seen, using tools specifically selected for handling an irresponsible colleague do prove influential. Let's return to the three scenarios that we examined at the start of the chapter and apply these tools to them.

■ An irresponsible and sloppy banker fails to provide his quality-conscious peer with the information she needs to complete her own work on time. The more conscientious colleague confronts her co-worker about his failure to meet the agreed deadline for delivering the information. This time she doesn't use arguments about quality, service standards, or basic courtesy. Instead, using a measured and firm tone, she tells him that she cannot complete her work without the information he owes her, and makes the point that she is sure he is aware of this fact. She explains that should she not have the information she needs in one hour's time she will need to take action. Without waiting for an answer she gets up and leaves his office. Then she goes to her desk and sends an email to her boss, an email which she copies to her irresponsible colleague and to his boss. In it she sets out the facts: that her colleague has failed to deliver key information to her on time and hasn't contacted her since the deadline passed; that she needs the information to complete her work for her own boss and cannot do so without the missing data; that she expects the information to arrive within one hour. Her colleague may well be difficult to deal with, even nasty, following his receipt of the email, but he will find it difficult to stall on delivering the data for very much longer, having been exposed to both his boss and her boss as deliberately obstructive. He may well scapegoat her behind her back, characterizing her as unreasonable and unprofessional, but he will need to deliver the missing information nonetheless.

■ An irresponsible research scientist receives an email from his more diligent accounts colleague pointing out that his recent questions about expense codes and costs have gone unanswered. The research scientist simply deletes the email and then ignores two subsequent follow-up messages which he retrieves from his telephone voice message system. When the accountant comes to his office to ask for the information face to face he does not make the mistake of assuming that the research scientist has good reasons for failing to answer his queries. Instead he assumes that he is being deliberately dilatory, and holds him accountable for his personal failure to respond to his three requests for information. He tells the research scientist that he is there to get the information he needs. He tells him that he will not be able to avoid dealing with him, and that should he fail to provide him with the information he needs, he will publish the quarter's accounts with a caveat saying that he has had no cooperation from the research scientist and that his figures are not included. The research scientist gulps. He knows that the report goes to everyone on the board. He complies with the request to provide the information.

■ A drug company saleswoman is confronted by her more assiduous peer who tells her that her client update reports are inaccurate, inconsistent, and poorly presented. She states that this state of affairs reflects badly on the sales team as a whole. However, the more assiduous peer decides that she is not willing to rework the reports no matter how bad a light they place the team in. She lets them go for circulation and goes home on time. Before she leaves she mentions to her colleague that issuing such a poor standard of paperwork reflects badly on the department, but it also harms her own reputation. Then she leaves it with her to decide whether or not she wants to take the risk.

In each of these cases an irresponsible colleague is faced with unpleasant consequences as a direct result of their negligent actions, and it is *this discomfort* – threatened or actual – that results in their choosing to amend their ways and address the issues before them. It is only when the consequences of their irresponsibility rest with *them*, and cause *them* pain, that they will do what they ought to have done in the first place.

YOUR INFLUENCING BEHAVIOR

We have been examining a range of situations in which an irresponsible colleague is called to account for their conduct by a more responsible colleague. You may now like to apply this material to your own working life. Identify a situation in which you were working alongside an irresponsible colleague, someone whose approach caused issues for you in your work. Bring the situation to mind, then answer the following questions about it. You can jot down your answers to each of the questions in the space below it:

■ What was the situation you have called to mind?

■ Thinking about that specific situation, what issues did your colleague's irresponsible conduct raise for you?

■ How did you attempt to influence your colleague at the time? To what extent was this strategy successful?

■ Should you find yourself in the same situation again what changes, if any, will you make to the way in which you seek to influence the situation?

So far we have been considering the impact of a colleague whose behavior is irresponsible on their more dedicated colleagues, co-workers, and managers. Now let's consider a different situation, one in which an irresponsible colleague has also secured the good opinion of senior and influential figures in the organization. Consider the following case study, which is set in a pharmaceuticals company.

CASE STUDY ELEVEN: MANAGING REPUTATIONS

The operations manager in a pharmaceuticals company is irresponsible and dilatory in his approach to his work. His team are highly motivated to do a good job, and regularly take it upon themselves to meet the deadlines and produce the outputs that he should be taking care of. They are quite comfortable doing this, taking pride in their performance and enjoyment from the quality of teamwork they display. Their manager is also regularly out of the office for long periods at a time, and they are used to keeping the workflow going whether or not he is in attendance in the department. When he returns from one of his long absences he always has a story to tell, about how he has been 'fighting for his team' or 'providing air cover.'

One day the team hear through the grapevine that their manager is up for a promotion and a significant pay rise. Two senior members of the team decide to speak to him about the rumor to see what is going on. They are worried that they might lose him to another department and have to work for another manager. Having spoken to their boss they report back to their colleagues. They state that his view of the situation seems to be that his reputation with his own boss is so effective that he has been selected for promotion. They report that he apparently didn't mention the work of his team when he accepted the offer of promotion, and neither did he acknowledge to them in the meeting they just had with him that they keep the department going while he is either absent from it at meetings or in his office. The two senior colleagues feel put out, and say so.

Over a period of weeks they and the rest of their team start to view their relationship with their manager differently. They begin to question whether their boss really does add significant value to their work. They begin to wonder whether he isn't actually very clever at leaving much of the responsibility to the dedicated people he has recruited into the team so that he can coast. They begin to realize that while he doesn't carry much of the load in the team, he is clever at taking all the credit for the work of the department. They think that the picture he paints to the wider organization does not reflect what actually goes on in the department, but has directly resulted in his being rewarded for their hard work. All this would be fine if he had acknowledged their part in his promotion. But he didn't, and the team thinks he is taking them for granted, using them even, and is promoting his own profile while they do all the work.

While none of the team want to let their work standards slip, they do want it to be known in the wider organization that it is they and not their manager who shoulder a lot of the responsibility for the work of the department. They also want their manager to acknowledge how much they do to keep everything running smoothly in his absence. There are a number of ways in which this group of people could respond to this situation. Let's explore three of them:

■ The team ask their two senior colleagues to go and speak with their manager again. They agree to do so. They go to his office and explain that the team are a little put out that he hasn't come to thank them for their hard work. While never going so far as to say they feel resentful that he hasn't acknowledged their contribution to his promotion, the two colleagues make it clear that the team expect their manager to speak with them. They are astonished to hear him say that he 'doesn't see the need.' They protest, pointing out more forcibly that the team often keeps the workflow going in his absence. Their manager becomes sharply angry and says 'I keep the reputation of the department afloat, you don't.' Then he orders his team members from the room.

■   The team members become sullen and resentful at what they see as their manager's mistreatment of them. They hadn't realized that he saw them as a soft touch, people he could take advantage of and use to advance his own prestige. They become hardened toward him, and while they never deliberately miss a deadline or fail to complete a task, several members of the team go home on the dot and put more effort into their private lives while putting less into their working lives. Eventually, errors do creep into the work of the team, and their manager is called to account by his boss for the mistakes and omissions made by his department.

■   The team reviews its options and decides that it will draw up a list of priorities and present it to their boss. They make it clear to him that they cannot complete all the items on the list, and that he must make a decision about which items to complete first and which to deprioritize. When presented with the list the manager puts the ball back into the team's court, saying that he wants their recommendation about prioritization. They counter by suggesting that he should make the call, as he is the one who needs to manage the reputation of the department to the wider firm.

The Opportunity to Influence

In this scenario a competent and dedicated operations team feel fed up that their work-shy and slippery manager takes the credit for their hard work while failing to give them the credit they deserve, either inside the department or with his bosses. They form the view that he presents their work as his, and spends time in the wider organization managing his profile and enhancing his reputation, while leaving them to shoulder the work unrewarded and unacknowledged.

They need to find a way to influence him to realize that his conduct is unfair on them and not that wise either. If they are able to influence him to amend his approach, they might be able to redress the balance somewhat, and achieve some kind of recognition outside of their department. If they are unable to redress the balance they may well find themselves becoming bitter and resentful that they carry the responsibility while their manager engineers a situation in which he gets the rewards.

Handling the Personalities

Let's explore the three instances to examine how the team seek to influence their manager.

The First Instance

In the first instance the team decides to appeal to their manager's goodwill. They set out to reason with him. Their influencing argument is that the team would like to be thanked for their hard work, but it falls very flat indeed. Their manager is distinctly unimpressed at being asked to tell his team that he owes some of his success to them and their efforts. He shuts the conversation down straight away, saying curtly that he 'doesn't see the need' to hold such a meeting. The two senior team members try again, aware that they are speaking for their colleagues whom they do not want to let down. They have to tread carefully as their boss is now riled. They say that it is they who keep the department going in his absence. On hearing these words their manager gets angry, and tells them in no uncertain terms that it is he and not they who keeps the reputation of the department going. These ruthless words crush the two senior team members and leave them with nowhere to go. They return defeated to their workstations.

Why did their appeal to their colleague's goodwill fail? Basically, this approach backfires on them because their manager doesn't have any goodwill toward them. He truly believes that he keeps the department going, and that his constant attempts to manipulate perceptions and engineer his own advancement outside the department are the decisive factor. He values these skills above any other, and definitely values them above the hard-working dedication demonstrated day in, day out by his team members. He treats their request for thanks and acknowledgement, which is something they would highly prize, as ridiculous and demeaning to him. He dismisses the suggestion out of hand. Having failed to even get a hearing, his two senior colleagues can now be left in no doubt that they are dealing with quite a ruthless man, someone who puts his own advancement above all other considerations, even facts.

However, his approach will not necessarily bear dividends for him. He *doesn't* give enough weight to the role of his team in his growing reputation. In fact he discounts their role, preferring to take considerable pride in his own calculating maneuvers. His foolishness is such that he doesn't realize that without his team's hard work he wouldn't be able to promote himself as he does. He doesn't make the connection between their willingness to go the extra mile for him, and the opportunity he has to present himself to his bosses as indispensable. In refusing to acknowledge their work, even by a round of drinks after work, he has mishandled his staff and potentially set himself up for a fall. Only time will tell just how his staff will react to their manager's hubris. Only time will tell how they will respond to his attempt to reduce their application and effort to less than important alongside his ability to manipulate his managers' perceptions.

The Second Instance

In the second instance the team withdraws its support of their boss, not completely, but enough that some work that would normally have been completed on time and to standard before his promotion announcement is done so no longer. This approach does have an impact on their manager, and is partially successful at influencing him. Over time, the outputs from the department tail off sufficiently that the manager has to have some uncomfortable conversations with his boss. However, he has to act carefully. If he allows his annoyance with his staff to result in him having a go at them it will go against him. He may be cross that his reputation has been adversely affected by their lowered standards of work, but he must demonstrate some empathy for the reasons behind their actions if he is to avoid alienating them further. He will need to handle this situation with much more maturity and respect for his team than he has managed to show so far. He will need to demonstrate his appreciation to his team on an ongoing basis if he is to repair the damage he has done to his reputation in their eyes, and thereby avoid further harm to his reputation outside the department.

The Third Instance

In the third instance the team decide to call their manager to account over his lack of respect for and appreciation of their work. They go about this task quite cleverly, too. They ask him to make a key decision, one that will affect what work they prioritize as important and what work they deprioritize as less important. They know full well that their manager isn't sufficiently on top of the workflow to know which tasks ought to take precedence over which other tasks. They also know that he is unlikely to agree to make the decision, and will probably require them to make it. When he does adopt this tactic they are ready for him.

They point out that it is he who has to manage the reputation of the department, and therefore his own reputation, to the wider organization. This is a brilliant thing to say, as it makes an explicit link between the right decisions being made at the right time within the team, and the manager's ability to enhance his reputation outside of it. He is completely undone, and is faced with a stark choice. He could take responsibility for making the decision, something that he doesn't feel equipped to do, but something that properly sits with him as the manager of the department. But he risks making the wrong choice, thereby potentially harming his reputation. Or he will have to admit to his staff that he needs them to make the right choice for him. He is cornered, and will have to admit to himself first of all that he needs his staff, before he can then set about offering them just rewards and praise. How he handles this issue will be key for him in his ongoing relationship with a team of people without whom he is stuck.

The Outcome

There is no right or wrong way to handle this situation. In the scenario an operations team need to influence their manager toward the view that he should publicize to the wider organization just how much excellent work they undertake on his behalf. They need to influence him to realize that withholding just credit from them will inevitably harm his relationship with them, and in the long run, will adversely impact the quality of work they do for him, which will in time affect his reputation in the wider organization.

The scenario presents three ways in which the team could tackle the situation. Either of the last two approaches could work, although in different ways. The crux of the matter is that the team is prepared to amend their approach and handle their work and their manager differently. Only if they approach their work in the same way after the promotion announcement as before it will their boss be likely to get away with his unconscionable irresponsibility toward them.

Conclusions

The lesson from this case study is that while an irresponsible colleague may well get away with their irresponsible conduct for long periods of time, as soon as the colleagues who are either knowingly or unknowingly enabling them in their irresponsibility realize the situation and alter their approach, the irresponsible colleague will have to change their behavior too. The question for the team members in the scenario is: what actions do they want to take to confront their manager given their own commitment to high-quality work and the fact that their own integrity precludes their producing shoddy and substandard work?

YOUR INFLUENCING BEHAVIOR

The previous example focuses on how a team come to realize that their manager is taking advantage of their work ethic and high-quality outputs. They realize that he is presenting their hard work as his without also acknowledging to them how much he values their work. You might like to apply the material to your own working life. Bring a specific situation to mind in which you felt that a colleague took the credit for your work, then answer the following questions. You can jot down your answers to each of the questions in the space below it:

■ Thinking about that specific situation, which colleague took the credit for your work? How did you find out about it?

■ How did you handle the situation?

■ How effective was this strategy at influencing your colleague not to repeat their behavior?

■ Looking back on it now, what changes would you like to make to your influencing strategy should you be faced with the same situation again?

SUMMARY AND NEXT CHAPTER

This chapter has focused on how to build influence with irresponsible colleagues. It:

■ Suggested that most of your colleagues will be well-intentioned and straightforward to deal with.

■ Highlighted the fact that a minority of colleagues will be purposefully shoddy, negligent, and irresponsible in their approach to their work, and in these cases, will not care what consequences their conduct causes for you or their other colleagues.

■ Recognized that some of these colleagues will also be skilled at manipulating the perceptions of their bosses, and may also actively seek to take the credit for work they have not done.

■ Explored how irresponsible colleagues will continue to get away with their behavior if you or their other colleagues cover for them or bail them out.

■ Proposed that the most influential way of handling an irresponsible colleague is to ensure that they feel some discomfort as a direct consequence of their actions.

■ Presented a set of effective influencing tools specifically designed for use with irresponsible colleagues.

■ Included an opportunity for you to apply the material to your own working life.

The next chapter takes the form of a narrative case study. The case study explores the issues involved when a well-respected technology manager chooses to leave an industry in which he has worked for ten years and move to another industry. He leaves behind an excellent reputation as a delivery-focused, influential member of staff, and joins a new employer where he needs to build credibility from scratch. The case study examines how he tackles this challenge. It focuses on the difficulties he encounters, the errors of judgment he makes, and the successes he has over a six-month period as he seeks to build influence with his new colleagues. The case study highlights how simply trying to replicate an approach that proves influential in one organization with previous bosses, team members, and internal clients, doesn't automatically prove effective when working with different bosses, team members, and internal clients in a different culture. It illustrates how learning to read a culture and understand what factors prove influential in it takes skill, judgment, and patience, as does learning to use behavior that proves to be influential with a new range of colleagues and co-workers.

CHAPTER 9

Fragile Alliances, Building a Reputation: A Narrative Case Study

INTRODUCING THE TECHNOLOGY MANAGER

An ambitious and technically adroit senior technology manager decides that he wants a new challenge. For the past ten years he has run a series of technology teams that design and install custom-made enhancements to the trading systems used by an investment bank. The technology manager uses a combination of the first, second, and fourth influencing styles. His approach to a project involves setting direction and being clear where the project is going; maintaining a steady focus on the quality and detail of the work; and keeping an eye out for opportunities to sell and market his team's achievements to his trading clients. The technology manager's somewhat pugnacious, delivery-oriented style works well in the robust and fast-paced banking culture, and his work is valued by his clients. His team members like working for him too. They appreciate his desire to develop them, be supportive of them, and remain loyal to them provided that, like him, they perform consistently well.

The technology manager takes pleasure in his work. He enjoys working with his team to design and deliver effective customer-focused projects. He benefits from a reputation as a team leader who finds neat solutions to tricky technology challenges, and does so without fuss and with considerable effort. The trading teams he supports like the fact that the technology manager doesn't waste their time. They like the fact that he is realistic about the disruption to their work that his team's redesigns and installations will inevitably create, and the fact that he respects the pressures that this places on them. They also like the no-nonsense way in which he speaks with them, translating what they cuttingly term 'techie-speak' into everyday language. They know where they are with him, and if they have a problem they know he will respond speedily to it and resolve it for them.

The technology manager is technically knowledgeable, and while quite willing to accept a brief to improve the capability of the trading groups his team supports, he is also willing to approach them with ideas that might create a competitive advantage for them. He is seen as that rare thing in a bank: a technologist with the drive and robust constitution required to handle the front office and make a positive impression with them, while also being an able and effective manager, someone whose team are loyal to him and respond well to his leadership.

The technology manager sees himself as pragmatic and realistic. He likes his focus is on creating an efficient team which is delivery oriented. He likes his energy and his drive. He thinks of himself as someone who 'will always make a decision,' and as someone who is willing to take on additional responsibility and acquire new projects to manage even when he and his team already have a full workload. He constantly looks for new ways to improve his team's effectiveness and efficiency so that they can add more value to the work of the trading teams they support.

However, the technology manager does not have easy relationship with his immediate boss, whom he doesn't rate. He takes an occasional wry dig at his manager and sometimes at the managers above him, and his team members are familiar with his frustrations. He sees the senior technology managers as gray corporate men and women, people who avoid responsibility and don't make decisions, people who leave issues unresolved and simply expect him and his team to remain effective despite the lack of clarity they periodically create. He gets particularly annoyed when his budgets are reduced or his team members are removed from the projects he has assigned them to without any consultation with him, and at these times he lets his feelings be known.

The technology manager also has periodic trouble working effectively with his peer group. His current peers are a notoriously difficult group of people to work with, being both adversarial and self-protecting in nature. He sees himself as different from them in two ways: he wants to do a good job, and he is conscientious. The technology manager takes what he does very seriously. He considers himself to be driven to deliver high-quality solutions, and being responsible and committed to his employer, he wants to spend his budget in as cost-effective a way as possible. He regards his peer group as being made up of slightly embittered men and women who lack his capacity for honest endeavor and want to get along by doing as little as possible while being paid well for doing it. Consequently, it is the technology manager who works later than they, it is the technology manager who steps in to rescue projects that they have failed to manage closely enough, and it is he who spends some evenings worrying about the direction and details of particularly high-profile cross-team projects.

HANDLING THE COMPLEXITY

One incident illustrates the technology manager's success at handling the complexities of his role particularly well. His team is deep into the development phase of a project to enhance a trading system when they run into trouble. One of their key suppliers lets them down, and it falls to the technology manager to explain to the head of equities sales that the timescales for the project installation will be put back by two weeks.

To the time-critical trading business head, this will sound like very bad news indeed. The technology manager arranges to meet him, goes to his office, and tells the head of equities sales that he is taking personal charge of the project. He says he is quite willing to go with the head of equities sales to meet his bosses and explain on his behalf why there will be a two-week delay. He watches as the impending angry outburst from the head of equities sales dissipates. His understanding of the parlous position this delay will put his client in with his bosses, along with his obvious commitment to making amends, circumvents the famously short fuse of the head of equities sales, and buys the technology manager the two weeks he needs.

The technology manager goes to the senior trading meeting with the head of equities sales and puts the case to them. He explains factually what has happened, states why there will be a two-week delay in completing the project, then outlines how those two weeks will be spent by his team designing further incremental improvements to the new trading system upgrade. He tells the assembled executives that the incremental improvements will add value to the system and make it even more beneficial to them upon its installation.

The head of equities sales is impressed with the technology manager's presentation. He is relieved that he doesn't have to deliver this bad news himself, and grateful that the technology manager has turned what appears to be bad news into very good news. He shakes the hand of the technology manager at the completion of the meeting. Two weeks later the improved installation commences.

TIME FOR A FRESH CHALLENGE: JANUARY

After ten years in the sector, and three years in his current role, the technology manager has built a reputation as an able and trusted advisor to the business. But he feels he has gone as far as he can in the role, and not wanting to take on the additional political element of a more senior role in his existing organization, he decides to move on. He doesn't want to become rusty and get into a rut, ending up like some of his peers, a bit cynical and sometimes slapdash in his work. He decides that he will make the move and go to work in another industry instead.

He decides to explore a number of opportunities and see what they have to offer him. However, he is clear that the role he wants will involve running an IT team to develop and implement technology solutions which will give his employer a cutting-edge advantage. He is confident that he will be able to replicate his current success elsewhere. He considers that his influence in his current team is derived from his desire to reward effective performance, his team members' personal loyalty to him, and his willingness to use his technical ability to set direction for their work. He hired many of his current team himself, and he thinks he will be able to replicate this leadership style with his new team easily enough. He fully expects a different group of technologists to respond to him just as well as his current team does.

He then considers the level of influence he enjoys with his current employer. He forms the view that his profile outside his department is derived from three distinct features of his style. The first is his effective use of his expert technology knowledge when handling his clients and team members; the second is his ability to build and sustain effective relationships and useful connections with his clients and co-workers; and the third is his reputation as a service-oriented, dedicated manager. He thinks that he will be able to replicate these approaches and build influence with his new colleagues as well. He is confident that he will be able to keep his technical knowledge updated, will be able to establish effective relationships straightaway in a new company, and that his style and character – as a pugnacious, hard-working, delivery-focused manager – will gain him political currency. He speaks to a series of search and selection firms, and outlines what he can offer to a new employer.

THE TECHNOLOGY MANAGER'S OFFER: FEBRUARY TO APRIL

The technology manager describes himself to the executive search firms he speaks with. He emphasizes his client-handling, team management, and leadership abilities alongside his technology knowledge and skills.

He tells the headhunting firms that he is well known for his ability to deliver effective solutions to difficult clients, and cites a number of instances where he has built robust relationships with challenging, demanding, and unreasonable trading groups.

He tells the executive search agencies that his influence comes from being able to deliver high-quality, effective solutions to pressurized clients in a service-oriented way. He explains that he commands quiet respect from the trading floor, has substantial influence with his clients, has the loyalty and backing of his team members, and is prepared to tell his boss how it is. He describes the three sources of his influence as being the effective relationships he builds with his clients and technology colleagues, his up-to-date technical knowledge, and his service-oriented style. He tells the executive search agencies that he is willing to take responsibility, always makes a decision, and enjoys working in fast-moving cultures.

After three months of searching he accepts a role running a technology team in the insurance industry, and resigns from the bank. He is excited and energized by the new challenge, and cannot wait to start his new job. He is confident that he will adapt well to the culture of the insurance firm, and expects that he will find his feet quickly. He is conscious that he is leaving behind an excellent reputation and significant level of client and team trust, both of which he greatly values. He is keen to replicate his success in his new role. His new boss, whom he meets during the interview process, promises him autonomy and latitude. She makes it clear that she expects the technology manager to run technology, and that, while she anticipates him keeping her informed, she will concentrate her time on her main responsibilities as chief financial officer.

The technology manager is not alarmed that his boss has little or no technological knowledge. He is pleased at the room for maneuver her hands-off style will afford him. He looks forward to working with his team without much interference from above. The technology manager thinks that the role is tailor-made for him, and goes on a two-week holiday with his family to recharge his batteries before starting his new job. It is early April.

FIRST IMPRESSIONS: LATE APRIL

During his first week in his new role the technology manager embarks on a round of talks with his clients, peers, and technology contacts. He meets his own senior team, their teams, and his four key clients.

He meets with the heads of human resources, underwriting, and risk management. He also has two meetings with his new boss.

He forms the view from these meetings that his colleagues regard his arrival positively, but he also thinks that they are not as frank with him as he would like them to be. On the occasions when he asks open questions he is disappointed at the lack of candor in the answers he gets, and forms the view that his colleagues are not used to being asked direct questions. He interprets their reactions at the time as evidence that they think they are being 'put on the spot.'

In his meetings with his key clients he makes a point of positioning himself as a responsive and proactive advisor. He tells them that he manages his team in an inclusive, open, and non-hierarchical way. He says that he is quality-focused and service-oriented in delivery. He tells them that he is keen to add value to the work of the businesses he and his teams support. He then asks them to outline to him their priorities so that he can begin to address them. He is surprised that none of his four key clients feels inclined to give him either a headline reaction or a detailed response to this question. Each of them deflects the question, or changes the emphasis of the conversation away from his chosen topic to a related one. But none of them supplies him with the information he needs, and none of them answers him directly. The technology manager is perplexed by their apparent lack of willingness to brief him on their requirements from him.

When he meets with his technology team, things don't go a whole lot better. He walks the floor of the technology office on his first day, and stops to speak to quite a few of his new team members. The atmosphere in the office is studious and hard-working, but not many people seem to be chatting, relaxed, or obviously enjoying what they are doing. The technology manager has not inherited a team before, and he realizes that he has some closed and reserved characters in the wider team, people with whom it will take time to build rapport.

He arranges a three-hour meeting for his senior team on the fourth day of his employment. He starts the meeting by telling his management team members that he sees them as the group of people who will handle the projects being undertaken by the department. He tells them that he sees his own role as primarily being about selling and marketing the achievements of his group to the business, while working with his team to identify new ways in which the technology team can support the work of the business. He says that he manages his team as a meritocracy, and rewards effort, commitment, and delivery. He tells them that he encourages the continual development of members of the group, and is ambitious for himself and his team. He says that he believes that listening is vital. He asks each person to outline what their values are, and what they would like to see the team doing over the next six months. The management team members answer these questions, but with a level of reticence that surprises the technology manager. He doesn't doubt their individual ability as managers or technologists, but he does doubt their willingness to contribute wholeheartedly to the team. He also begins to question their attitude to him.

In his second meeting with his boss towards the end of his first week, he decides to test the waters and venture an opinion or two about the perceptions he has formed. In the end he doesn't have to look for an opportunity. His boss asks him outright how he has found his first week. He says that he has learned a lot in a short time, that he has had a round of productive talks with his management team and key clients, and has gleaned plenty of food for thought. Then he says that he is adjusting to a less forthright and more modest culture than he is used to, but thinks he will find his feet quickly enough. His manager replies that what really matters is his ability to ensure a high-quality service to the business and effective responses to business priorities. She tells him that he has a talented team of people who are keen to learn and are good at providing early communication about significant technology risks or enhancements that might benefit the business. The technology manager feels reassured, and goes home for the weekend in good spirits.

LOSING INFLUENCE AND POWER: EARLY MAY

Over the next two weeks the technology manager gets down to work, but is surprised at how difficult he finds it to get things done. His team members are industrious and busy. When he asks for input or ideas from them he gets responses, but he forms the view that his team members respond with a subtle reluctance that he finds hard to pin down. No one is deliberately uninterested or evasive, but the technology manager feels frustrated at the lack of impetus and pace around the team.

He is also frustrated that each of his courtesy calls to his clients goes unreturned. In his previous role he was used to getting airtime with the business whenever he requested it, but here he finds it difficult to secure even one response. He leaves a second message with each of his key clients, saying that following his introductory talk with them he'd like to arrange a short follow-up meeting. He is again disappointed that he doesn't get any replies. He decides to pay a visit to one of his clients in his office, and on arriving, is told by his PA that he is busy and cannot be disturbed. The technology manager asks her to relay the message that he would like a few minutes of the manager's time, and leaves.

The technology manager is not used to be treated like this, and finds the experience disabling. He questions what is behind the apparent lack of interest in his requests for time from his clients, and unable to find any answers, starts to doubt himself. He is not used to a situation where his messages are ignored, and he finds the reality of this hard to deal with. Without any true allies in his new employer, he goes home and speaks with his partner about his consternation that he cannot seem to get the attention of the senior people with whom he is used to dealing.

FEELING CONFUSED: LATE MAY

The technology manager concentrates on getting to know his team and their projects. He familiarizes himself with the platforms and software used by the insurance firm. Being technically adept he enjoys this aspect of his work, and after a few days in which he is fully occupied working with his team and their projects, he receives a call from the PA of one of his key clients offering him a ten-minute meeting with the business head that afternoon. The technology manager accepts the offer and goes to the meeting.

After preliminary exchanges about how he is finding his new role, the technology manager tells his client that he would like to work with him and his team to identify ways in which the technology team could add value to his business. His client leans back in his chair, takes a breath, and says that he will talk with his team and get back to him. His demeanor is laid back, and while not casual, definitely at odds with the eager and slightly intense style of the technology manager. The technology manager decides not to press the issue, and stands up. He walks to the door, and as he reaches it, his client looks up from his work. The business head says that he used to call the technology manager's predecessor when he had a problem. Then he picks up his phone and dials a number. The technology manager leaves the office feeling bemused.

He starts to worry that the job is not working out. His specific concerns are that his clients do not seem to have a sufficiently well-developed understanding of what he can offer them to enable them to take advantage of the work he and his team could do for them. He also worries that his upfront and action-oriented style of doing things might be coming over as too in-your-face to the cerebral and low-key senior insurance managers he has met. The technology manager wonders if he hasn't misjudged the culture of his new employer, and feels concerned that he might not know how to operate effectively in this understated and discreet firm. Indeed, he wonders if he will enjoy working in it at all.

He thinks that there is a discrepancy between how the role was sold to him at interview, how his new boss described it to him during his first week, and how he experiences it. He worries that while his team members are fully engaged on maintenance, redesigns and research, the technology team is not regarded as a proactive business partner by the wider organization. He also thinks that many of his team members are under-stimulated and stagnating. He believes that his talented team could tackle much more complex projects, and worries that he will find it hard to hold on to his more skilled and experienced people if he is unable to offer them higher-level work.

He starts to think constructively about what he could do to build influence in a workplace where he is fast starting to feel invisible. It's not that he wants to be important, more that he wants to make a contribution, and is concerned that, if he cannot raise his profile and the profile of technology team as a whole, it won't be possible for him to have the impact he would like. His usual methods of building influence are not working in this culture, and frustratingly, his tried and tested approach actually seems to lose him credibility rather than help him gain it. Normally, all he would need to do would be to pick up the phone to a client, tell him that he has an idea he would like to talk through, and he would be offered an early opportunity to do so. In this firm, the opposite happens. His calls are regarded as a nuisance by his clients, who either don't respond at all, or do so only to make the point that they would rather he left it to them to call him.

He realizes that the issue does go to his own personal conduct and style, but he forms the view that it also goes to the reputation of the technology team as a whole. He thinks that his client colleagues do not understand just how much of a cutting-edge advantage he and his team could provide them with. He thinks that they see the technology team as an overhead, a group of people they have to maintain on-site, but a group of people who are only useful when things go wrong. It's almost as if they are worried about involving technology any further in their work, for fear of getting into territory they don't understand.

The technology manager feels dismayed at how things are turning out. This isn't the job he thought he had signed up for, and he realizes that if he is to make a go of it and build influence, he will have to do a lot of work to change perceptions. He will need to change the perception of the role that technology can play in the business. He will need to build influence with each and every one of his clients, educating them about how to work productively with him and his team, teaching them how to get best value from him, and how to involve him in their decisions from early on so that he can become a true partner in their businesses. The technology manager thinks he will have his work cut out if he is to achieve any or all of these aims.

He doesn't know if he has the skills to pull off this influencing challenge, or the inclination to try. His own strengths are around creating momentum for change, managing projects to completion, and selling and marketing achievements. He doesn't know if he can embark on an influencing process designed to alter the way his senior colleagues regard his group and its work for the firm. He also feels angry that he has moved from a role where his work was valued, into a role where it isn't. He is annoyed with himself for not asking more questions during the interview process, and for putting himself in this position. He had been looking for a new challenge, but he hadn't counted on the type of challenge he now faces. He had wanted to work with new people and new technology issues. He hadn't counted on working for a firm which doesn't make the most of its existing technology or its technology team, and which doesn't seem to value or trust the service that its lead technologist wants to provide.

A CLEAR CHOICE: EARLY JUNE

The technology manager considers either complaining about a misleading interview process or resigning from his role, but he does neither. He thinks that it would be pointless to complain, and might further undermine his reputation if he does so. He also considers that it would be detrimental to his career to leave a new role after little over a month.

He decides that he has a clear choice. He can remain in the role and seek to build influence with each of his new clients and colleagues sufficiently that in a year or 18 months' time, he might have a job he thinks worth doing; or he can tread water in the role as it currently is, and seek to move to another employer in two years' time. He decides that his personality and character preclude him from treading water.

He simply couldn't do it. He thinks that he would hate coming to work quite quickly if he adopts this approach, so he determines to rein in his frustration and seek to build influence with his new colleagues, so that he can work toward creating the kind of profile he needs to enjoy his new job.

GOING THROUGH THE MILL: LATE JUNE

But this isn't an easy thing for him to do. The technology manager decides to run a series of seminars to introduce his new colleagues to the ways in which the technology team can add value to their businesses. He explains the idea to his boss, designs a one-hour format, produces slides for it, advertises it in the building in which he works, and considers asking one of his team to deliver it. However, he decides that it would be more time-effective to run the session himself, as he has the information at his fingertips and is used to giving presentations. He schedules three seminars, and provided they go well, plans to hold further sessions in the firm's other offices. He is disappointed when only a handful of people attend the first seminar, and even more disappointed to realize that most of them are quite junior managers.

The technology manager is angry with himself. He thinks he has wasted his time, as well as set himself up for quite a public humiliation. He considers that someone with his seniority should not have put himself into a position where he has wasted time and money on an in-house seminar that few people attend. He regards his seminar as a failure, and cancels the subsequent two scheduled events.

The technology manager decides that he needs to approach this task from a different angle. He puts on hold his idea to produce and distribute a brochure outlining the role that technology could play in helping the business achieve a competitive advantage. Frustrated that his first idea hasn't worked, and that he now thinks his second won't work either, the technology manager decides that he must build influence with his key colleagues one at a time.

ESTABLISHING CONTACT WITH THE BUSINESS: JULY

The technology manager opens a dialogue with a series of key clients on an individual basis. He selects the first client he wants to meet with, the head of business services, and mulls over how best to approach the meeting. This colleague is one of the clients who didn't respond to his phone calls, and this time the technology manager is determined to secure a meeting with her. He wants to send her the clear message that he and his team have something valuable to offer her business. He forms the view that this client is probably unaware of the value that technology could add to her team's work, and wants to address this situation.

He calls the head of business services' PA and requests ten minutes in her diary. His tone is brisk and businesslike, and he says that he has something to discuss with her that he thinks will interest her. Her PA calls back later that day with a date at the end of the following week. The technology manager asks if there is anything sooner, and after some discussion, agrees to a five-minute meeting at the end of the next working day. He regards the meeting as key not only to improving his state of mind, but also to his plans to enhance the profile and reputation of the technology group as a whole. Aware that his key clients will likely swap notes about him with one another, he decides to handle this first meeting in a way that builds influence with this particular client so she can spread the good news.

The technology manager wants to set the right tone at the meeting. He doesn't want to be too informal or matey, and he doesn't want to be too pushy or earnest. He also doesn't want to come over as thinking that what he has to offer will automatically be seen as valuable by his client simply because he thinks it is. He wants to get the balance right between conveying his own conviction that he has value to add to her business, and letting her make up her own mind on the matter. It is her decision after all, and the technology manager thinks that the way in which he presents his offer to her is as much a key selling tool as is the substance of the offer itself. He wants to conduct the meeting in a crisp, clear, businesslike fashion in which he comes over as low-key, dedicated, helpful, and task-focused.

He goes to the meeting and after brief introductions decides to get down to business straight away. He starts by saying that he is meeting all his key clients one at a time. He then says that he is keen to identify ways in which he and his team can add value to her business. He pauses for a few seconds, giving her time to digest this information, before adding that he doesn't expect an answer straight away, and that if she would like to think it through she can get back to him when he is ready. As he speaks his tone is gentle rather than punchy, and he presents his words as an offer. He is aware that his client is sitting very still while he speaks, and appears to be appraising him. He thinks that she is forming a judgment about him, in terms of both what he is offering and how he is offering it.

The technology manager maintains eye contact with his colleague and keeps his demeanor open as he waits for a reply. He is very aware that in offering her the opportunity to tell him how he can be of greater service to her, he is asking her to consider involving him more closely in her team's work. The technology manager recognizes that to his risk-averse and technologically uneducated colleague, this might be a difficult thing to do. He realizes that she doesn't have much technical knowledge and, should she involve technology more closely in her work, would inevitably be dependent on the skill and judgment of the technology manager and his team, people she doesn't know very well. She would have to be prepared to trust someone whose style is counter-cultural to hers, and to hand over a considerable degree of control to him and his team if she is to gain any benefit from working with them. He is sensitive to the fact that she might find the prospect of doing this quite daunting.

So the technology manager waits for a few seconds to let his colleague mull it over. Then, when she still hasn't spoken, he says that he will leave it with her and if he hasn't heard from her in a couple of weeks he will assume that there isn't anything that she needs from him. He is careful to use the word 'need' rather than 'want.' He uses the same gentle but firm tone as he says these words, and hopes that they convey to his client that he knows he has something valuable to offer her, but is also leaving the ball in her court.

The head of business services considers this statement for a few seconds, then asks the technology manager to join her at her next management team meeting. The technology manager is delighted, and accepts the invitation, which is for a meeting in just under a month's time. He is frustrated at what he considers as yet another delay, but decides to use the intervening time to address a number of issues in his own team.

GAINING GROUND: JULY

Over the next three weeks he spends time speaking with his team members one by one. His aim is to build influence and trust with each member of his team, sound them out on the prospect of becoming more involved in the day-to-day work of the business, and determine what skills gaps he needs to close.

One member of the team, in particular, has caught his eye. This team leader is someone who the technology manager has noticed chats a lot more than her colleagues, and can often be seen walking across the office floor to talk to someone on the other side of the room. The technology manager thinks that this team member is one of the more inter-personally skillful members of his team, and wants to talk to her about her role. He asks her to come into his office for a meeting. After a few minutes talking about current workloads and priorities, the technology manager prepares to bring up the issue he wants to talk about.

He considers that his team member's periodic wandering around the office is actually a symptom of a deeper problem rather than the actual issue itself. Rather than tell her that he has noticed her wasting time, being idle, or spending a lot of time chatting around the office, he decides to find out what is behind the behavior he has observed so he can address the real issue. Changing to a more considered tone, he says, 'I've noticed that you get up and walk over to talk to colleagues a lot more than most other people in the team. Is everything OK with you?'

The team member doesn't reply at first. She sits quietly judging whether or not she can be candid. She decides to test the water. She says that she finds the office 'a little quiet.' Heartened, the technology manager decides to play her words back to her to encourage her to expand a bit further. He says, 'Too quiet for you?' and waits for a response. His team member tells him that she is used to a bit more variety, and finds the quiet atmosphere in the office rather inhibiting. The technology manager asks her what role she is used to performing. She replies that she is used to working closely with a team, and finds her current solitary role uncomfortable. The technology manager stores this useful information away in his mind, and tells her that he understands her dilemma and will see what he can do to change things around.

FLAWED APPROACH: JULY

He then turns his attention to another of his team members, this time a member of his senior team who was argumentative and surly with him at the half-day meeting he arranged at the end of his first week. He asks this team manager to come into his office, and gets down to business straight away. He tells her that he wants to build a high-performing management team, and that he would like her to be part of that team. He tells her that he thinks she has sound technical ability and could play a bigger role in the department. He pauses to let his words sink in. Then he says, 'I see you everyday in the office handling complex and challenging work very well. I observe you handling your junior colleagues with tact and patience, and I think they learn from you. But, with me, you can become truculent and angry for no apparent reason. This concerns me, and I am worried that you might treat me in this oppositional way simply because I am senior to you in the firm.'

The technology manager says all of this in a low-key, non-confrontational tone, but he emphasizes the words 'oppositional' and 'senior' to make it clear that he has made a link between her unhelpful behavior and his organizational authority. He thinks she might not have understood this link herself, and he wants to spell it out for her. His demeanor remains open as he speaks and his voice and eye contact remain steady. He doesn't want to embarrass or humiliate her. He doesn't want to handle the meeting in a way which would result in her working less effectively for him. Rather he wants to reflect back to her how she is coming across, and give her an opportunity to rethink her behavior. It is a difficult balance for him to strike. He forms the view that the team member does not realize that she reacts on impulse to his authority, and consequently opposes him on instinct, rather than because she has thought about the issues and come to a considered view about them which happens to differ from his. The technology manager wants to give her a chance to recognize her behavior for what it is, alter it for the better, and use different behavior from that moment onwards.

Having reflected back to her how she comes across to him, he lets the silence continue. He wants to be sure that his words have been absorbed. Then he tells her that he would like to review the situation again in a month or so. Again, he uses a low-key tone, and is careful not to sound menacing or angry in conveying this information. Then he ends the meeting and lets his team member leave his office. He watches her return to her desk deep in thought.

ESTABLISHING CREDIBILITY: LATE JULY

The technology manager meets with two more of the three outstanding clients over the next few weeks, and while he doesn't gain as much ground with them as he did with the head of business services, he does manage to open a dialogue with each of them. As a result of these discussions he comes to an important conclusion. He forms the view that establishing influential connections in this firm is all about having key pieces of information. He comes to the conclusion that he is not sufficiently in the know, and that if he is to build any substantial credibility with his client base, he must address this issue.

He forms the view that having influence in this firm is not primarily about character, values, or displaying a service-oriented disposition. It's not even about whom he knows or what degree of trust he has developed with these people. These factors proved influential with his last employer, but in this firm they don't seem to matter so much. What clearly does matter is in the first instance, having up-to-date information about what is going on organizationally, and in the second instance, knowing in what way to position this knowledge with other colleagues so that it proves pivotal. One instance proves this to him conclusively.

He arranges to meet with the third of his four clients for a ten-minute conversation just before lunch on a Friday afternoon. The technology manager arrives on time for the meeting, which is being held in his client's office. But his client isn't there, and his PA tells the technology manager that he is attending the business steering committee meeting and will be back shortly. The technology manager waits in his client's office. On returning, the client apologizes for being a few minutes late and makes the point of telling the technology manager that he can't afford to leave the meeting early as it is his main opportunity to keep up-to-date with the key trends in the business and the decisions that will be made as a result of those trends. He adds that all the business heads attend the meeting, which is held once a month. The technology manager has the presence of mind to comment, 'Sounds like *the* meeting to be at?' To which his colleague replies, 'Without a doubt. Now what can I do for you?'

The technology manager decides that, without a seat at that table, he is unlikely to build the influence he needs. No matter how service-oriented, charismatic, well-connected, or technically able he is, without a place at that meeting he will not have the opportunity to enhance his profile or make the kind of contribution he would like to make. The technology manager decides that he must find a way to be invited to that meeting, and makes a mental note to discuss the issue with his boss. He considers this move to be a risk, because he is highly alive to the fact that his boss has not yet suggested that he attend the meeting, at which she is a regular participant. Nor indeed has she drawn his attention to just how important a meeting it is for any manager who wishes to have influence. The technology manager does not regard his boss as a political animal. He does not think she has deliberately excluded him from the meeting, or purposefully omitted to tell him about its profile in the firm. He thinks it is much more likely that she hasn't thought about it from his point of view. She attends it as a matter of course in her capacity as chief financial officer (CFO), but he decides that she won't have realized how key a place at that table could prove to be for him, so hasn't brought it up with him.

Nonetheless, the technology manager is concerned about how his boss might react to his wish to attend the business steering committee. Even if she doesn't want to exclude him from it, he is astute enough to realize that she might not welcome his attendance at it either. He judges his moment and then approaches her. He suggests that it might be a good idea if he participates in an upcoming business steering committee meeting in his capacity as head of technology. His boss asks him why he wants to attend, and he says that it would be a useful way to understand in more detail the evolving priorities of the business. He says that he would value the opportunity to learn more about his client base and what they are seeking to achieve in the market, so that he can identify ways in which he can help them achieve their goals.

His boss considers the suggestion. Then she says that if he can get an invitation to the meeting she would welcome his participation in it.

SELLING HIMSELF: LATE JULY–AUGUST

The technology manager attends the business services management team meeting and listens closely to the discussion. It centers on ways in which the business should respond to recent market changes and upcoming government legislation. The technology manager identifies two clear opportunities to make enhancements to the systems that support the business, and briefly outlines them to the meeting. He emphasizes the positive outcomes for the business, and secures enough interest that he is asked to put together a more detailed specification for the two proposed projects. As the meeting ends he considers saying to his client that he would value an opportunity to attend the business steering committee with her, but desists. He decides that he needs to take it one step at a time, and frustrated at what he regards as the slow speed of progress, doesn't think the time is quite right to ask for an invitation to the meeting.

He goes back to his team and asks the bored and frustrated team member whom he spoke to a few weeks earlier to work with him on putting the proposals together. Two weeks later the proposals are accepted, and the technology team is asked to design and implement the two enhancements to the system. The technology team manager forms two separate project teams to handle the work, and asks the

team member who worked with him on the proposals to head up one
of them.

BUILDING INFLUENCE: AUGUST

The technology manager has now been in his new role for four months.
He has made progress, albeit slowly, and has built some influence with
some key clients. But he still doesn't enjoy anything like the level of
profile or influence that he would like to have after four months of
employment.

Then the technology manager sees an opportunity. He asks his
business services client if he can meet with her team leaders to outline
in more detail what the new software will do for them. She agrees,
and a meeting is set up at lunchtime over sandwiches. The technology
manager decides to use the meeting to impress upon the team leaders
how useful the new technology will be to them and their teams, and
what benefits it will bring to their customers. He also wants to open up
a conversation with them about what other incremental improvements
to the systems they might welcome. He takes his interpersonally adroit
team member with him.

He sets an open tone from the start of the meeting, outlining the scope
and the benefits of the new software projects. He describes the timescale
for the work, and explains the details of the post-implementation
support his team will provide for them and their teams. His business
services colleagues listen but remain largely silent in the meeting. They
appear to be absorbing the information, but he cannot tell what they
think about the proposals. So he asks them. A few people murmur that
the proposals sound OK, but no one ventures anything useful.

The technology manager forms the view that there is something
that is not being said. So he asks them what is their biggest bugbear
with technology. In the silence that follows he thinks that each person
is judging whether or not to speak, and if they do speak, what to
say. He lets the silence continue, and maintains eye contact with each
person one by one. He simply waits for someone to say something.
Eventually, one team leader does. The following 30 minutes prove
very useful for the technology manager and his colleague. They hear
a number of specific complaints about the platform and the current
software. They hear a number of anecdotes about how requests
for information go unanswered, and listen to a certain amount of
frustration and annoyance at the lack of speedy engagement from the
technology team to escalations.

Having set himself the task of building influence with the business, the technology manager now realizes that he will also need to influence his own department to adopt a more service-oriented culture. He is disquieted to hear the feedback he has received, and concerned that it has taken him so many months to hear it.

GAINING A REPUTATION: SEPTEMBER

The software enhancements for business services are completed, and the technology manager attends the subsequent management team meeting. He asks for feedback on the software, and hears mainly good news. He is disappointed to hear that, despite his work with his own team, there is still a level of dissatisfaction with the length of time it takes some of his team members to respond to calls for assistance.

The technology manager says he will personally investigate and get back to the business services managers involved. At the end of the meeting he tells the head of business services that he would like to attend the business steering committee. He explains that he would like to be able to work with her and the wider business to understand what the future trends in the market will be, so that he can identify in advance possible ways in which technology enhancements could provide the firm with a competitive advantage. He boldly asks his client to introduce him to the meeting. He asks her to outline to the meeting the benefits to her team that the recent software enhancements have created. She agrees, and at last, the technology manager thinks he is getting somewhere toward his aim of building influence in the firm. The next business steering committee meeting is three weeks away. He puts his thinking cap on, determined to use this opportunity to the fullest.

MAINTAINING INFLUENCE: OCTOBER

The technology manager plans for his first appearance at the business steering committee. He is aware that he still has much to do if he is to establish the level of influence he wants in the firm, and position the technology team as a valued partner to the business. But at least now he has a chance. After six months of looking for opportunities to build his profile, he is finally going to participate in *the* meeting to attend if he wants to keep abreast of what is happening in the firm. Attending it is simply the first step. Then he has to do the real work, that of conducting himself in a way which builds credibility with the senior colleagues at the meeting, results in them inviting him back, and over time, trusting him enough to involve him in their business plans and proposals.

The technology manager recognizes that he has come a long way in the six months. He has had to employ new and different influencing behavior with his clients and team members. He has had to look actively for influencing opportunities outside of his department so that he can patiently build his profile. Never entirely comfortable with the culture of the insurance firm, the technology manager has nevertheless learned to rein in his naturally straightforward and decisive style, and adopt a more unobtrusive and inconspicuous demeanor instead. This has taken time, energy, and resolve. He has worked hard to convince his clients that he deserves the opportunity to work more closely with them and their businesses.

Above all, he has adjusted to and fitted into a prevailing culture which at first he simply did not understand. He has demonstrated considerable courage. He has tried new and unfamiliar influencing approaches, and has kept experimenting until he discovered which influencing tactics work most effectively with which colleague. Now that he has a seat at the most important meeting of all, the technology manager needs to take advantage of the opportunity he has carefully crafted, or all his hard work will be in vain.

CONCLUSIONS

This case study has followed the fortunes of a technology manager as he learns how to understand and adjust to the alien culture of a new employer. It has demonstrated that it can take time to get to grips with a new culture, and to learn what behavior does and does not prove influential in the new firm. And it has highlighted the value of building steady sponsorship and support over a period of a few months. What are the key lessons the technology manager learned?

The technology manager learned that:

- The approach he used at the bank to such good effect does not prove influential in the insurance firm, which has a different culture and in which different factors prove decisive.
- The onus is on him to adopt a new and more influential approach if he is to convince his new colleagues that he has something valuable to offer them.
- He needs to take the time to build influence slowly and steadily with selected key, influential people.

- He needs to use different influencing tools with different people, and recognize that making subtle changes to his approach can make all the difference when building influence with certain colleagues.
- It is worth his while cultivating the sponsorship of key clients, who will likely share their positive opinion of him with their peers.
- It takes time to build a reputation. He has to search assiduously for the right opportunity to build his profile and sell his team to the business.
- Earning the right to attend the business steering committee is not an end in itself. It is only the first step. His next challenge is to use that opportunity wisely.

Those of you who would like to explore the influencing themes of this case study in greater detail might like to refer to pages 111–114 in Chapter 8 and to the whole of Chapter 9 of *Managing Politics at Work: The Essential Toolkit for Identifying and Handling Political Behaviour in the Workplace* (by Aryanne Oade, published by Palgrave Macmillan, 2009). These pages define and illustrate seven different sources of organizational influence, such as information influence and relationship influence, which are highlighted in this narrative case study.

Aryanne Oade

To tell me about your experiences of gaining and retaining influence in your workplace, and to explore options for developing further skills in these areas, visit www.oadeassociates.com

References and Recommended Reading

REFERENCES

How to Use This Book

A. Oade (forthcoming) *Handling Clients Effectively: How to Initiate, Sustain and Retain Long-Term Customer Relationships*, Palgrave Macmillan.

Chapter 2: Influence, Power and Responsibility

A. Oade (2009) *Managing Politics at Work: The Essential Toolkit for Identifying and Handling Political Behaviour in the Workplace*, pp. 73–129, Palgrave Macmillan (ISBN 978-0-230-595415).

Chapter 3: Four Sets of Influencing Values

Everett T. Robinson (1995) *Why Aren't You More Like Me? Styles and Skills for Leading and Living with Credibility*, HRD Press (ISBN 970-0-87425-970-3).

Chapter 9: Fragile Alliances

A. Oade (2009) *Managing Politics at Work: The Essential Toolkit for Identifying and Handling Political Behaviour in the Workplace*, pp. 111–14 and 121–29, Palgrave Macmillan (ISBN 978-0-230-595415).

RECOMMENDED READING

D. Goleman (1994) *Working with Emotional Intelligence*, Bloomsbury (ISBN 0-7475-4384-4).

Daniel Goleman's down-to-earth and insightful book applies Emotional Intelligence theory to the workplace. It outlines a set of emotional skills, all of which can be learned, to help you become a more effective communicator, influencer, and manager of workplace relationships.

Everett T. Robinson (1995) *Why Aren't You More Like Me? Styles and Skills for Leading and Living with Credibility*, HRD Press (ISBN 970-0- 87425-970-3).

There are a number of behavioural styles models on the market, with related books and materials. This paperback book is a thorough, informative and readable examination of one of the more comprehensive behavioural styles theories, Personal Style Indicator, devised by one of its co-authors. The book includes the short form of the Personal Style Indicator questionnaire.

A. Oade (2009) *Managing Politics at Work: The Essential Toolkit for Identifying and Handling Political Behaviour in the Workplace*, Palgrave Macmillan (ISBN 978-0-230-595415).

This practical book will help you to recognize and manage your own and other people's political behaviour at work. It will help you develop the political management skills you need to maximize your influence at work. The book highlights how to handle situations where, if you don't respond effectively to other people's political tactics, you will lose personal power and credibility, or fail to gain influence in the first place. In particular Chapters 6–9 focus on how to work effectively in situations where you have to get things done in tandem with colleagues.

M. Bragg (1996) *Reinventing Influence: How to Get Things Done in a World Without Authority*, Financial Times/Prentice Hall (ISBN 978-0-273-623137).

This is an older book but it's still still good value. It contains some useful self-awareness exercises and helpful ideas on influencing in different organizational cultures.

Index